D1519690

Language and the Self
in D. H. Lawrence

Studies in Modern Literature, No. 68

A. Walton Litz, General Series Editor

Professor of English
Princeton University

Keith Cushman

Consulting Editor for Titles on D.H. Lawrence
Professor of English
University of North Carolina at Greensboro

Other Titles in This Series

Language and the Self in D. H. Lawrence

by
Diane S. Bonds

UMI Research Press

Ann Arbor / London

A portion of chapter 1 originally was published in *Proceedings of the Conference of College Teachers of English* as "D. H. Lawrence and the Paradox of Language." A portion of chapter 2 originally appeared in *The D. H. Lawrence Review* as "Miriam, the Narrator, and the Reader of *Sons and Lovers.*" A portion of chapter 4 originally appeared in *Essays in Literature* as "Going into the Abyss: Literalization in *Women in Love.*" Grateful acknowledgment is made to the editors of these journals for permission to reprint.

For permission to quote extracts from the works of D. H. Lawrence, grateful acknowledgment is made to Laurence Pollinger Ltd., the estate of Mrs. Frieda Lawrence Ravagli, and Viking Penguin Incorporated.

Produced and distributed by
UMI Research Press
an imprint of
University Microfilms Inc.
Ann Arbor, Michigan 48106

Library of Congress Cataloging in Publication Data

Bonds, Diane S., 1946-
Language and the self in D. H. Lawrence.

(Studies in modern literature ; no. 68)
Revision of thesis (Ph.D.)—Bryn Mawr, 1978.
Bibliography: p.
Includes index.
1. Lawrence, D. H. (David Herbert), 1885-1930—
Knowledge—Language and languages. 2. Lawrence,
D. H. (David Herbert), 1885-1930—Philosophy.
3. Self in literature. 4. Speech in literature.
5. Languages—Philosophy. I. Title. II. Series.
PR6023.A93Z569 1987   823'.912   86-30727
ISBN 0-8357-1789-5 (alk. paper)

For Greg and Hannah Rose,
with love

Contents

Acknowledgments

This book originated in research completed at Bryn Mawr College in 1978; its present critical orientation derives from my participation in a 1980 National Endowment for the Humanities Summer Seminar at Yale University under the direction of J. Hillis Miller. Thomas H. Jackson of Bryn Mawr and Professor Miller have generously extended their encouragement and support of this project into the present. Though my study does not make direct reference to manuscript and typescript materials housed by the Humanities Research Center of the University of Texas, those resources strengthened my conviction that it is important to look carefully at Lawrence's language; and I wish to thank the staff of the HRC for their cooperation over several summers. Southwest Texas State University and Agnes Scott College provided me with financial support in the form of faculty research grants. Most recently I have been grateful for suggestions from Keith Cushman and for material aid in producing my manuscript provided by Candler School of Theology and Emory University. William L. Hedges, my undergraduate teacher from Goucher College, has been a continuing source of support. My great debt to my immediate family is recorded in the dedication to this volume.

Editions and Abbreviations of Works by Lawrence

A   *Apocalypse and the Writings on Revelation.* Ed. Mara Kalnins. The Cambridge Edition of the Works of D. H. Lawrence. New York: Cambridge UP, 1980.

CL I   *The Letters of D. H. Lawrence.* Vol 1. Ed. James T. Boulton. The Cambridge Edition of the Letters and Works of D. H. Lawrence. New York: Cambridge UP, 1979.

CL II   *The Letters of D. H. Lawrence.* Vol. 2. Ed. George J. Zytaruk and James T. Boulton. The Cambridge Edition of the Works and Letters of D. H. Lawrence. New York: Cambridge UP, 1981.

K   *Kangaroo.* 1923. New York: Viking, 1960.

P   *Phoenix: The Posthumous Papers of D. H. Lawrence.* Ed. Edward D. McDonald. 1936. New York: Viking, 1968.

P II   *Phoenix II: Uncollected, Unpublished, and Other Prose Works by D. H. Lawrence.* Ed. Warren Roberts and Harry T. Moore. New York: Viking, 1970.

P/F   *Psychoanalysis and the Unconscious and Fantasia of the Unconscious.* 1921, 1922. New York: Viking, 1960.

R   *The Rainbow.* 1915. New York: Penguin, 1976.

SL   *Sons and Lovers.* 1913. New York: Penguin, 1976.

SCAL   *Studies in Classic American Literature.* 1923. New York: Viking, 1964.

WL   *Women in Love.* 1920. New York: Penguin, 1976.

Abbreviations will be used only where the context does not make the work cited obvious.

Prologue

This study began as an effort to understand D. H. Lawrence's conception of language. Even though Lawrence makes relatively few explicit remarks about language, his critical writings and his major novels—*Sons and Lovers, The Rainbow*, and *Women in Love*—imply a great deal, and so I undertook an effort of explication to uncover in those works Lawrence's "theory" of language, insofar as he could be said to have one. So ambivalent is this writer toward his medium that I soon became practiced in a certain kind of reading, in that deconstructive operation that Barbara Johnson describes as "the careful teasing out of warring forces of signification within the text" (*The Critical Difference* 5). That Lawrence's writing should thus educate the reader—at least a reader in our current critical climate—is not surprising when one considers the parallels between some of his critical statements and statements from our contemporaries writing about deconstruction:

> The curious thing about art-speech is that it prevaricates so terribly, I mean it tells such lies.... And out of a pattern of lies art weaves the truth.... The artist usually sets out—or used to—to point a moral and adorn a tale. The tale, however, points the other way, as a rule. Two blankly opposing morals, the artist's and the tale's. Never trust the artist. Trust the tale. The proper function of a critic is to save the tale from the artist who created it. (Lawrence, *Studies in Classic American Literature* 2)

> The de-construction of a text does not proceed by random doubt or arbitrary subversion, but by the careful teasing out of warring forces of signification within the text itself. If anything is destroyed in a deconstructive reading, it is not the text, but the claim to unequivocal domination of one mode of signifying over another. (Johnson, *The Critical Difference* 5)

> To do this [to deconstruct a Freudian text, or to see how it deconstructs itself] is not to trust Freud the man but to give oneself maximum opportunity to learn from Freud's writing by supposing that if this powerful and heterogeneous discourse is at one point operating with unjustified assumptions, these assumptions will be exposed and undermined by forces within the text that a reading can bring out. (Culler 169)

> [E]very work of art adheres to some system of morality. But if it be really a work of art, it must contain the essential criticism on the morality to which it adheres.... The degree to

> which the system of morality, or the metaphysic, of any work of art is submitted to criticism
> within the work of art makes the lasting value and satisfaction of that work. (Lawrence,
> "Study of Thomas Hardy" [P 476])
>
> [G]reat works of literature are likely to be ahead of their critics. They are there already.
> They have anticipated explicitly any deconstruction the critic can achieve. (Miller,
> "Deconstructing the Deconstructors" 31)
>
> The value and force of a text may depend to a considerable extent on the way it deconstructs
> the philosophy that subtends it. (Culler 98)

Unlike our contemporaries, Lawrence seems to grant the "unequivocal domination" of "one mode of signifying over another" (of the "tale" over "artist"), but the more important point here is that he shares with the other writers quoted a recognition that language is powerfully wayward, ultimately eluding the control of any "master" but providing wealth, for those who struggle with it in good faith, greater than any writer can consciously exploit—and greater than any critic can exhaust. Great literature is heterogeneous and ultimately self-interrogative; its meaning is forever unsettled and unsettling. Lawrence, Miller, Johnson, and Culler all indeed imply that the greatness of literature derives from its heterogeneity. Deconstruction, as Barbara Johnson's description hints, is a way of respecting and appreciating the heterogeneity of texts. When I sought Lawrence's implied theory of language, I inevitably encountered the self-deconstructive or self-interrogative forces in his writing: his critical writing directed me to seek such forces, and I found them in the play of his heterogeneous metaphors for human utterance.

To trace the movements or operations of those metaphors is one purpose of this book. A related purpose is to show that the kinds of tensions, conflicts, or ambivalences that occur with regard to language recur with regard to the issue of selfhood. Lawrence links language and selfhood in his Foreword to *Women in Love*:

> Man struggles with his unborn needs and fulfilment. New unfoldings struggle up in torment
> in him, as buds struggle forth from the midst of a plant. Any man of real individuality tries
> to know and to understand what is happening, even in himself, as he goes along. This
> struggle for verbal consciousness should not be left out in art. It is a very great part of life. It
> is not superimposition of a theory. It is the passionate struggle into conscious being. (WL
> viii)

"The passionate struggle into conscious being" and the role of language in this struggle are twin concerns in Lawrence's writing. In the foreword to *Women in Love,* his identification of the "struggle for verbal consciousness" both with the individual's efforts "to know and to understand" and with "the passionate struggle into conscious being" implies that conscious being is determined by language. Yet Lawrence's writing offers considerable and obvious resistance to this idea. His preoccupation with what he terms "blood-consciousness" is but one sign of a desire to circumvent language in the quest for conscious being. Such a desire constitutes a paradox in one committed to the struggle for verbal consciousness, a paradox that it is one aim of this book to explore.

The Critical Tradition

> It seems as if an appreciation of Lawrence must always be made in a half-antagonistic way. (Potter 151)

> Rousseau is one of the group of writers who are always being systematically misread.... [T]he implied function of most critical commentaries ... is ... to do away at all costs with [the] ambivalences [inherent in all literary and some philosophical language].... When, especially as in the case of Rousseau, the ambivalence is itself part of the philosophical statement, this is very likely to happen.... in Rousseau's case, the misreading is almost always accompanied by an overtone of intellectual and moral superiority, as if the commentators, in the most favorable of cases, had to apologize or offer a cure for something that went astray in their author. (de Man 111–12)

Though I do not believe that Lawrence has been "systematically misread" in the ordinary sense of the term, I do believe that he should be classified with de Man's Rousseau as one of those "most enlightened" writers about whose works "a recurrently aberrant pattern of interpretation" (de Man 111) has arisen. The aberration in the case of Lawrence has recently been summarized by Avrom Fleishman:

> A nonspecialist coming to D. H. Lawrence studies must be moved by the intensity with which his ideas are debated but surprised at how little is made of his stylistic achievements. When attention is paid, it is usually to deride or defend the universally acknowledged *badnesses*—the purple passages, the swatches of slack dialogue and careless narration, the lapse into self-indulgent vituperation. (162)

While Lawrence studies are increasingly appreciative of the value of stylistic and rhetorical analysis of Lawrence's work, critics have most often treated his writing as if it were principally a tissue of ideas or of represented experiences, not a tissue of linguistic signs, except, as Fleishman suggests, where some supposed ineptitude or embarrassment forces an apologetic or defensive acknowledgment from the critic. The "overtone of intellectual and moral superiority" that de Man mentions pervades, in more or less subtle forms, the body of criticism of Lawrence. A characteristic example occurs in Baruch Hochman's *Another Ego: The Changing View of Self and Society in the Works of D. H. Lawrence*: "Despite eccentric habits of language and idiosyncratic turns of thought, Lawrence maintains a consistent interest in the problems of self and society..." (xi). Hochman, like many of Lawrence's critics, offers a patient and careful reading; he is far from condescending in his tone; yet there is an attitude of intellectual superiority involved in presuming that Lawrence's interests and ideas can be understood apart from his so-called "eccentric habits of language."[1]

The aberration in Lawrence studies is, to me, the degree to which Lawrence's verbal idiosyncrasies have *failed* to command critical scrutiny. Indeed, a subtheme in the criticism is the necessity of eliminating concern about precisely those idiosyncrasies, eliminating it so that "criticism"— understanding, evaluation, appreciation—may proceed. F. R. Leavis begins his pioneering chapter on *Women in Love*: "I have not always thought *Women in Love* one of the most striking works of creative originality that fiction has to show—I have not always thought it successful enough to make such judgment reasonable" (175); Leavis was disturbed in his early readings by an "insistent and overemphatic explicitness, running at times to something one can only call jargon," but by the time he writes *D. H. Lawrence: Novelist,* he finds this feature of the novel "a fault that [he does] not . . . see as bulking so large in the book as [he] used to see it" (179). The process by which readers come to admire what they once found inept or repulsive is also the subject of some remarks of Mark Schorer concerning the same novel: "The intention of *Women in Love* is so tremendous, so central to our lives, that we must for our own sakes make an effort to tolerate it. I say tolerate for the reason that I have known almost no readers who, on *first* reading, did not find it either opaque beyond endurance, or tiresome, or revolting" ("*Women in Love* and Death" 44–45). Graham Hough similarly argues that "most readers . . . will find it hard to be convinced by the complicated relations of Gudrun and Gerald, Ursula and Birkin, on the plane of ordinary human action and character"; Hough goes on to write that "the obscurity and mystery" that exercise many readers "lessen on re-reading. All Lawrence's novels tend to carry more conviction in the ordinary social-naturalist sense the more familiar they become. Which only means that his idiom has to be learned" (75).

Certainly the concessive terms with which these critics grant Lawrence his greatness constitute an effort to anticipate and dispose of problems readers may encounter in first approaching Lawrence's works; but as one critic has quipped in connection with this issue, "We can get used to anything" (Bickerton 66). The remarks of Leavis, Schorer, and Hough confirm, it seems to me, the truth of de Man's contention that the "aberrant pattern of interpretation" in the case of highly ambivalent and philosophically complex writers like Rousseau (and, I believe, Lawrence) is closely allied to, indeed may result from, "a blindness of critics with regard to their own insights" (111). Learning Lawrence's idiom, cultivating tolerance—these likely involve those processes by which, according to de Man, critics "blind" themselves in order to see: doing away with ambivalences, "reducing them to contradictions, blotting out the disturbing parts of the work or, more subtly ... manipulating the systems of valorization that are operating within the texts" (111) so that the writer's works become "readable."

In his deconstruction of Derrida's deconstruction of Rousseau, de Man concludes that such blindness is unavoidable; it is "the necessary correlative of the rhetorical nature of literary language" (141). Critical blindness is, one might say, the inevitable and necessary result of the encounter between the multivalent language of literature and what Edward Said has called the mind's "need for unity" (41). Lawrence's critical prose, implicitly if not explicitly, rehearses some of the issues found in contemporary criticism; for example, *Apocalypse* provides telling affirmation of the difficulties of literary interpretation with which de Man grapples.[2] Yet much of the criticism of Lawrence operates on the basis of what de Man would call a "naive" assumption, a belief discredited, as we shall see, by *Sons and Lovers* and the novels immediately following it: the belief in the possibility of a seamless unity of thought and language, in the possibility of "organic wholeness" of literary expression. Not only do Lawrence's masterpieces, as I argue, call those presuppositions into question, but his critical prose, in particular the passage I have already quoted from "Study of Thomas Hardy," places high value upon precisely those self-interrogatory dynamics of literary texts, dynamics to which Lawrence's critics have systematically "blinded" themselves: the dynamics of self-deconstruction, in contemporary critical parlance.

I am *not* suggesting that critics have blinded themselves to all self-critical elements in Lawrence's writing. F. R. Leavis (213–21) and Frank Kermode (66), most notably of many, have sensitized us to the ways in which Lawrentian texts like *Women in Love* test the ideas proposed in them. What I am suggesting is that there are certain presuppositions so crucial to the conduct of orthodox Lawrentian studies that critics have avoided looking at the ways in which Lawrence's writing interrogates their validity. An example of such a tenaciously held view is the common attitude that Lawrence and James Joyce represent antithetical poles of modernism.[3] Such a view becomes less tenable once one acknowledges that Lawrence's writings are in some ways as profoundly shaped as Joyce's by an awareness of the power of the linguistic system that enmeshes them both.

Neither do I mean to suggest that I have not exercised my own sort of blindness. The degree to which the following discussion refuses to engage issues important to other Lawrence critics is testimony to my own choice of an enabling, selective blindness. In reading the novels, for example, I am not so much interested in what characters' experiences mean as I am in the ontological and metalinguistic implications of the texts' language. To read Lawrence in this way is not to diminish the importance of his characters' quests for fulfillment. It is to say that the greatness of his masterpieces lies in more than their representation of certain kinds of human experiences (a dimension that, in any case, has been rather fully examined in the criticism); their greatness also lies in their implicit dramatization of important questions about the constitution of language and the self. To say this, of course, is to return to the arena of "ideas," but it is to arrive there through acknowledging a nonreferential dimension in Lawrence's writing which undermines the representational or mimetic dimension, reminding us that his novels are textures of words.

1

Lawrence and the Paradox of Language

Lawrence acknowledges his paradoxical relation to language when he writes, "I'm like Carlyle, who, they say, wrote 50 vols. on the value of silence" (CL I: 504). Such a statement encompasses certain antinomies in his attitudes toward language. He often uses metaphors of energy, activity, and process to suggest that language is spontaneous, creative spiritual emanation or what he calls "utterance."[1] Utterance, by bringing forth the "new unfoldings [that] struggle up . . . in [the individual], as buds struggle forth from the midst of the plant" (WL viii), fosters conscious being or, to use Lawrence's characteristic organic terminology, the flowering of the self. Somewhat at odds with this organic view of language, however, is a recognition that the external linguistic system is a system of rules and signs. As such, language can entangle the self in a web or, to use another of his metaphors, confine the self in a prison of preexisting form. Thus language might be said both to liberate the self (from what Lawrence calls "the unconscious" into conscious being) and to imprison it.

The Organic Self and Symbolism

Lawrence's unsystematic and oblique elaboration of this paradox is inextricable from his discussions of the unconscious and of consciousness in *Psychoanalysis and the Unconscious* and *Fantasia of the Unconscious*. In the former work, he repudiates the Freudian notion of the unconscious, calling it "the cellar in which the mind keeps its own bastard spawn" (9), nothing more than the "whole body of our repressions" (10). Objecting to the idea that the "contents" of the unconscious are in any way touched by the mind, he insists that the unconscious is "pristine," prior to consciousness of any sort: it is "the first bubbling life in us" (13), "the fountain of real motivity" (9). Lawrence's elaborate renamings of the unconscious in *Psychoanalysis* draw upon both religious and biological terminology; the unconscious is, at one extreme, "the soul" (15) and, at the other, "the first nucleus [of the fertilised egg] subdivided" (36). To forestall the criticism that he defines "the unconscious" so loosely that it "is only another term for life," he writes:

[L]ife is a general force, whereas the unconscious is essentially single and unique in each individual organism. . . . It is always concrete. In the very first instance, it is the glinting nucleus of the ovule. And proceeding from this, it is the chain or constellation of nuclei which derive directly from the first spark. . . . The nuclei are centres of spontaneous consciousness. It seems as if their bright grain were germ-consciousness, consciousness germinating forever. (42–43)

The passage insists that the unconscious is anterior to consciousness and that the unconscious and consciousness are inseparable as motive and motion, ideas reinforced in Lawrence's writing by his reliance on the model of organic growth in discussing human consciousness. When he writes that the nuclei of the nerve cells (where he "locates" the unconscious) seem to be "germ-consciousness, consciousness germinating forever," he posits the idea that the unconscious is a seed. As such, it is the motive of development in the individual "towards a florescent individuality" (P/F 26). That blossom of individuality is nourished by consciousness viewed as the "sap of our life, of all life" (P 18). "Primal consciousness," comprising the first, premental impulses of the soul or unconscious toward self-manifestation, "remains as long as we live the powerful root and body of our consciousness. The mind is but the last flower . . ." (P/F 74). Such metaphors suggest the following paradigm: the unconscious is a seed whose only purpose is to unfold itself and flower; consciousness is both the unfolding and the flower—root, stem, bud, blossom, and sap that flows through all.

The flowering, or the "incarnation and self-manifestation" of the soul, is "the whole goal of the *unconscious* soul: the whole goal of life" (P/F 42), according to Lawrence's pseudopsychoanalytic essays. A process occurring in all living organisms, it is, in any person "of real individuality," identical to "the passionate struggle into conscious being." Language seems to have value for Lawrence primarily as it serves this process, and it does so in "utterance." Lawrence uses that term to designate the "outering" of essence, to denote both verbal and nonverbal activities that express the soul or life-force of individual organisms.

Thus in the descriptive essay, "Flowery Tuscany," crocuses leap "with flowery life and utterance" (P 50). Indeed, all utterance is a kind of flowering. In "Education of the People," Lawrence names Shelley and Parnell as supreme "utterers" and asserts that the activity of "the great man, or the most perfect utterer," can constitute the supreme blossoming of "the tree of human life"—can give expression to an entire nation or race (P 609–10). Even sartorial creativity can be a flowering, an utterance. In the same essay, Lawrence writes of a woman of the future who, schooled to know her own soul, makes her own clothes, "evolving and unfurling them in sensitive form, according to [her] own instinctive desire. She puts on her clothes as a flower unfolds its petals, as an utterance from her own nature, instinctive and individual" (P 652). In these passages, the term "utterance" and metaphors of flowering point to the same activity: what Lawrence would call the incarnation and amplification of the soul, the realization of the unique nature contained *in potentia* by the seed of the unconscious.

The metaphors of flowering confirm Lawrence's implication in the Foreword to *Women in Love* that verbal activity has the creative function of bringing forth conscious being or the self. The Foreword to *Fantasia of the Unconscious* not only endorses the idea but also provides more specific clues to the nature of the struggle for verbal consciousness:

> This pseudo-philosophy of mine—"pollyanalytics," as one of my respected critics might say—is deduced from the novels and poems, not the reverse. The novels and poems come unwatched out of one's pen. And then the absolute need which one has for some sort of satisfactory mental attitude towards oneself and things in general makes one try to abstract some definite conclusions from one's experiences as a writer and as a man. The novels and the poems are pure passionate experience. These "pollyanalytics" are inferences made afterwards, from the experience. (57)

The two kinds of writing, "passionate" and analytic, correspond to two stages in the process of verbal consciousness, the latter to mental consciousness, the former to something that precedes intellectual apprehension. Lawrence recognizes the mind's engagement in the process of imaginative composition when he writes that the mind "transmutes ... creative flux into a certain fixed cipher" (P/ F 46). Yet the passage from *Fantasia* partly implies that the poems and novels *are* untranslated flux: they "come unwatched," they actually "*are* pure passionate experience" (emphasis added) and not simply the product of it. In short, they seem to emanate directly from the soul or unconscious while the "pollyanalytics" are "deduced," abstracted from the creative flow. Lawrence is not so much distinguishing literary modes here as he is defining the *felt* relationship of words and ideas to two stages of consciousness. In "pure passionate experience," words (and the ideas they represent) are felt to be consubstantial with the creative flow of the unconscious; in abstract analysis, ideas (and the words that represent them) are perceived as entities disengaged from creative flux.

The truth value that Lawrence accords to creative flux—to the sap of dynamic consciousness—is clear in many of his works. *Studies in Classic American Literature,* for example, gives powerful voice to the belief that the unconscious has the power to generate spontaneously the words that give it "truthful" expression. Assuming that his "proper function" as critic is to "save the tale from the artist who created it" (2), Lawrence attempts to expose the "under-consciousness" of American literature—that is, to make explicit the great passional truths that American writers of the past produced but, to his mind, dodged. Lawrence's critical enterprise thus bespeaks a belief in the truth and potency of "art-speech" as unconscious emanation. When he writes of two "blankly opposing morals, the artist's and the tale's" (2), he implies that however deliberately a writer orders his or her words in accordance with a moral or intellectual purpose, the activity of the unconscious—the truly creative principle in the writer—will be at odds with that purpose and will record itself in the words that come to the writer.

Art-speech has the power to express the unconscious because it is symbolic. Like many of his romantic predecessors, Lawrence insists upon the symbolic—as opposed to the allegorical—nature of literary discourse. The premium that Lawrence places upon the notion of symbol is plain from the following passage: "Symbols are organic units of consciousness with a life of their own, and you can never explain them away, because their value is dynamic, emotional, belonging to the sense-consciousness of the body and soul, and not simply mental" (A 48; P 295).

Organic, dynamic, emotional—these key terms of value in Lawrence's own critical writing characterize his definition of symbols. The implication, common in romantic critical discourse, that symbols unite perception and feeling, object and subject, is supported by a comment from the first version of *Studies in Classic American Literature*: "Art speech is ... a language of pure symbols. But whereas the authorized symbol stands always for a thought or an idea, some mental concept, the art-symbol or art-term stands for a pure experience, emotional and passional, spiritual and perceptional, all at once" (qtd. in Armin 40).[2] Unlike the static, conventional symbols of allegory, the symbols of art-speech are dynamic. Not only do they integrate into a synthesizing image some of the conflicting impulses that constitute dynamic consciousness; they also have the power to generate or alter dynamic consciousness. As Lawrence writes in his Introduction to Frederick Carter's *The Dragon of the Apocalypse,* symbols "stand for units of human *feeling,* human experience. A complex of emotional experience is a symbol. And the power of the symbol is to arouse the deep emotional self, and the dynamic self, beyond comprehension" (A 49; P 296).

Lawrence's conception of symbols as "organic units of consciousness with a life of their own," as "art-terms" the meaning of which can never be explained away, constitutes an effort to imagine a kind of literary discourse that is inexhaustible and dynamic, invulnerable either to petrifaction or decay. But in his insistent conceiving of utterance as spontaneous, creative spiritual emanation, Lawrence at times seems almost to deny the preexistence of language. To the extent that he relies on metaphors of generation and organic growth in discussing consciousness, he promotes the fiction that the unconscious actually gives birth to the language through which it finds incarnation. This seeming denial of the preexistence of language, however, is actually a sign of Lawrence's deep awareness of the determinative power of the linguistic system. It is precisely this awareness that leads him to write in *Studies in Classic American Literature,* of the "subterfuge" of art, for the writer's imprisonment in a moral or intellectual scheme that denies passional truth is to a large extent a result of such imprisonment in language.

The Threat of Fossilization and the Prison of Language

To speak of such imprisonment is merely to draw out the implications of Lawrence's metaphors in *Psychoanalysis of the Unconscious,* where he likens consciousness not only to a flowering but also to "a web woven finally in the mind from the various silken strands spun forth from the primal centre of the unconscious" (42). The web corresponds to mental consciousness or the mind, which is not only "the last flower" of the unconscious but also "the terminal instrument of the dynamic consciousness": "It prints off, like a telegraph instrument, the glyphs and graphic representations which we call percepts, concepts, ideas. It produces a new reality—the ideal" (P/ F 46). The domain of mental consciousness, the ideal is not coextensive with the realm of consciousness in the broadest sense—that is, with the realm of "true consciousness" or "dynamic consciousness." Rather the ideal is but a product of such consciousness.

The ideal does, however, seem to be coextensive with language conceived of as both *langue* and *parole,* as both the linguistic system *and* all actual manifestations of that system. Lawrence's identification of language with the ideal can be seen in loose syntactical structures that classify words and ideas together ("the words and thoughts and sighs and aspirations that fly from [man]" [P 534]) and in his fondness for "the Word" as metaphor for the idea or the ideal, as in *Psychoanalysis and the Unconscious,*" where "the idea" and "the Word" become interchangeable terms (P/ F 46, 47). Because Lawrence refuses to make any clear distinction between words and ideas, his definition of the idea might serve just as well as a definition of the word or of speech or of writing: "an idea," he writes, "is just the final concrete or registered result of living dynamic interchange and reactions" (P/ F 119).

This definition encapsulates many of the oppositions in Lawrence's writing about language and consciousness. On the one hand, as we have seen, Lawrence treats words, apprehended as inextricable from evolving consciousness, from "living dynamic interchange and reactions," in terms of metaphors suggesting energy, activity, and process. He characterizes their energy as "vital" or "dynamic"; the processes in which they participate he likens to organic growth. But on the other hand, words viewed as "concrete or registered results," as discrete entities having their being in mental consciousness, he treats in figures suggesting fixity, rigidity, organic death. The power that such words can exercise is "mechanical."

So threatening is the mechanical power of the ideal that Lawrence writes, "The Ideal is *always* evil, no matter what ideal it be. No idea should ever be raised to a governing throne" (P/F 119). As "another static entity, another unit of the mechanical-active and materio-static universe" (P/F 46), the idea is capable of assuming a pseudovitality of its own, and in so doing, it threatens to subvert the process of dynamic or true consciousness which it mimes:

> "The word became flesh, and began to put on airs," says Norman Douglas wittily. It is exactly what happens. Mentality, being automatic in its principle like the machine, begins to assume life. It begins to affect life, to pretend to make and unmake life. "In the beginning was the Word." This is the presumptuous masquerading of the mind. (P/F 47)

Against the danger that words and ideas may take on an illegitimate autonomy or authority, Lawrence insists upon the insubstantiality and ephemerality of human utterance: our "words and thoughts and sighs and aspirations... are so many tremulations in the ether..." (P 534). They have substance only in the sense that tools or instruments have material substance, that is as "*appliances* which we can use for the all-too-difficult business of coming to our spontaneous-creative fullness of being" (P/F 48).

The danger that these mere "appliances" might "be raised to a governing throne," that these mere "tremulations" might assume substance and arrogate the function of the unconscious in directing human consciousness, is particularly acute in the case of literary tradition; for the language of literature, one might argue, is the language that most successfully imitates the motions of the soul and which may, therefore, most easily delude us into believing in its authority. Lawrence elaborates this possibility in his Preface to Harry Crosby's *Chariot of the Sun*, where he presents a parable of "the history of poetry in our era":

> Man must wrap himself in a vision, make a house of apparent form and stability, fixity. In his terror of chaos he begins by putting up an umbrella between himself and the everlasting whirl. Then he paints the under-side of his umbrella like a firmament. Then he parades around, lives and dies under his umbrella. Bequeathed to his descendants, the umbrella becomes a dome, a vault, and men at last begin to feel that something is wrong. . . . Then comes a poet, enemy of convention, and makes a slit in the umbrella; and lo! the glimpse of chaos is a vision, a window to the sun. But after a while, getting used to the vision, and not liking the genuine draught from chaos, commonplace man daubs a simulacrum of the window that opens on to chaos, and patches the umbrella with the painted patch of the simulacrum. That is, he has got used to the vision; it is part of his house decoration. (P 255–56)

As utterance, the language of the poet—or any literary artist—has the liberating force, and can even act with violence, to slit open the vaulted roof of tradition, to break through the conventions that make a poet and his readers go "bleached and stifled." Yet, paradoxically, the language of literature is the very material of the literary tradition or "the simulacrum"—the paint, plaster, daubed patches that ornament the painted vault; it in fact constitutes the vault itself. Painted to resemble "a glowing open firmament," it is nonetheless "all simulacrum, innumerable patches, Homer and Keats, annotated and with glossary" (P 256).

If such petrifaction and decay are the end of all utterance in Lawrence's organicist account of the path of language, then whether utterance takes the form of literary expression or more ordinary discourse, it must perpetually renew itself. As Lawrence writes in *Fantasia of the Unconscious*, the "idea...must rise ever fresh, ever displaced, like the leaves of a tree, from out of the quickness of the sap..." (119). Language and thought are alive—active and creative—only insofar as they deliver the "still unborn speech, still unknown thoughts" with which the soul or unconscious is "for ever charged" (P 608). This burden discharged, the potency of words dissipates, and they can renew themselves only in the sense that they can provoke "new living utterance." Lawrence makes this plain in his foreword to *Fantasia*, where he refers to a preglacial civilization and the wisdom it supposedly has passed down to us in "half-forgotten symbolic forms" (55):

> ...I have no desire to revive dead kings, or dead sages. It is not for me to arrange fossils and decipher hieroglyphic phrases.... The soul must take the hint from the relics our scientists have so marvellously gathered out of the forgotten past, and from the hint develop a new living utterance. (56)

"Ritual, gesture, and myth-story," the forms in which ancient wisdom is remembered, are "relics" and "fossils," petrified forms of past utterance which can be seen as possessing vitality only as they engage a living soul in the present.

The Fall into Allegory

The notion that utterance must perpetually renew itself poses, of course, particularly difficult problems for the literary artist: what kind of language can a writer choose that will retain the vitality, the quickness, that Lawrence associates with the act of utterance? One answer is offered by Lawrence's theory of art-speech in its valorization of symbols—and of a symbolic conception of language. Another approach to the problem is represented by his treatment of the reader's role in revitalizing literature. When Lawrence writes in his Foreword to *Fantasia of the Unconscious* of developing "a new living utterance" from the fossils and relics gathered from the past, he describes a model of creative reading which informs his two book-length critical studies, *Studies in Classic American Literature* and *Apocalypse*.

In these two works, whose composition was separated by almost a decade, Lawrence employs similar metaphors to describe the texts he scrutinizes. In *Studies in Classic American Literature* he argues that many masterpieces of American literature replicate the divided structure of the American psyche wherein an emergent "under-consciousness" struggles against a repressive surface consciousness. Lawrence's metaphors play in various ways upon the opposition of surface and depth and upon the idea of layers or strata:

> [T]he Americans refuse everything explicit and always put up a sort of double meaning. They revel in subterfuge. They prefer truth safely *swaddled* in an ark of bulrushes, and deposited among the reeds until some friendly Egyptian princess comes to rescue the babe. (viii, emphasis added)
>
> [W]e read old European inference *over the top of* Poe or Hawthorne. (1, emphasis added)
>
> Art has two great functions. First, it provides an emotional experience. And then, if we have the courage of our own feelings, it becomes a *mine* of practical truth.... But we've never dared *dig* the actual truth out.... (2, emphasis added)
>
> You have got to pull the democratic and idealistic clothes off American utterance, and see what you can of the dusky body of It *underneath.* (8, emphasis added)
>
> An artist usually intellectualizes *on top,* and his dark under-consciousness goes on contradicting him *beneath.* (26, emphasis added)
>
> You *must* look through the surface of American art and see the inner diabolism of the symbolic meaning. (83)

All of these passages implicitly link *Studies* with Lawrence's last book, *Apocalypse,* which displays the same concern with textual surface and depth. Lawrence uses archaeological metaphors to describe the text of Revelation:

> It is one book, in several layers: like layers of civilisation as you dig deeper and deeper to excavate an old city. Down at the bottom is a pagan substratum, probably one of the ancient books of the Aegean civilization: some sort of a book of a pagan Mystery. This has been written over by Jewish apocalyptists, then extended, and then finally written over by the Jewish-Christian apocalyptist John: and then, after his day, expurgated and corrected and pruned down and added to by Christian editors [scribes] who wanted to make of it a Christian work. (A 81)

The metaphor of a ruined city or civilisation is elided into a second one, that of something like a palimpsest, a stratified textual "structure [which must be read] vertically, as well as horizontally" (85). Lawrence extends the metaphor of palimpsest to the work of orthodox Christian commentators, viewing their commentaries not as separate entities so much as the topmost layer of the stratified textual structure that he calls Apocalypse. The authors of these works, according to Lawrence, "want to have their cake and eat it.... [T]he Apocalypse is a veritable heathen feast for them. Only they must swallow it with pious appearances" (85). Works of orthodox textual exegesis, like the work of the apocalyptists who wrote over the "pagan substratum" of Revelation, attempt to suppress or disfigure the pagan subtext that bears the great cosmic symbols of Apocalypse, symbols that Lawrence greatly reveres. Of one such work, R. H. Charles's *A Critical and Exegetical Commentary on the Revelation of St. John* (1920), Lawrence writes: "Archdeacon Charles admits that the seven stars in the right hand of the 'Son of Man' are the stars of the Bear, wheeling round the Pole, and that this is Babylonian: then he goes on to say 'but our author can have nothing of this in mind' " (83). Orthodox Biblical criticism is thus a structure of concealment which paradoxically admits into the text the pagan elements that it attempts to suppress: it "swallow[s them] with pious appearances" (85).

The parallel between Lawrence's description of the means by which Christian scribes and editors suppressed the pagan subtext of Apocalypse bears a striking resemblance to Freud's analogy, in "Analysis Terminable and Interminable," for repression and other defense mechanisms. Freud writes of

> various methods . . . for making [an undesirable] book innocuous. One way would be for the offending passages to be thickly crossed through so that they were illegible. In that case they could not be transcribed, and the next copyist of the book would produce a text which was unexceptionable but which had gaps in certain passages, and so might be unintelligible in them. Another way . . . would be . . . to proceed to distort the text. Single words would be left out or replaced by others, and new sentences interpolated. Best of all, the whole passage would be erased and a new one which said exactly the opposite put in its place. (23: 236)

Short of completely erasing the text and substituting one that said exactly the opposite, the Christian scribes and commentators, according to Lawrence, employed all the methods mentioned by Freud to make the Bible and in particular Revelation "innocuous": they "expurgated, or twisted into meaninglessness," "snipped out" or "stuck in," "smeared over," and did their best to erase or "cover up the pagan traces" in order to make "this plainly unchristian work passably Christian" (A 86).

The parallel between Lawrence and Freud underscores the role that Lawrence assumes in *Apocalypse* as recoverer of repressed materials. In his book, he refuses to protect any longer the Christian allegorical meaning that he claims was "verbally trodden" into his consciousness as a child "like innumerable footprints treading a surface hard, but the footprints were always mechanically alike, the interpretation was fixed, so that all real interest was lost" (A 59). Lawrence's effort is to uncover the "pagan traces" partly erased by Christian clerics and to restore to the traces their pre-Christian meaning or force.

A theoretical question arises, however, in connection with this effort. In presenting the notion of a stratified text, Lawrence never makes any distinct demarcation between the text of Revelation itself and Christian commentary;

thus he justifies the extension of the metaphor of strata to his own commentary. That Lawrence does not thus extend his own metaphor provokes an important question: what is to prevent his text from becoming just another repressive layer in that palimpsest he is calling Apocalypse? It is especially significant, in this regard, that he gives his own work the same name that he uses to refer to Revelation. In so doing he implies some awareness of the problem. And, in fact, his critical procedures in *Apocalypse* implicitly confront, though they never resolve, the difficulty.

The difficulty is one that also informs *Studies in Classic American Literature,* where the problem is that in his readings of American literature he may simply be substituting one "morality" or "metaphysic"—one ideal superstructure—for another. It might indeed be argued of *Studies* that in excavating or bringing to light the dark subtext of the classics he studies, Lawrence is actually *superinscribing* a morality of "blood-consciousness" or "dark-consciousness" upon the outworn morality or idealism he so deplores in the works he discusses. For example, in his chapter on Crèvecoeur, Lawrence finds in the author's letters, beneath the idealistic "stuff about nature and the noble savage and the innocence of toil, etc.," truly poetic "glimpses of actual nature" (26). Crèvecoeur "gives the lie to Innocent Nature"—to nature sentimentalized, idealized, romanticized, or "writ large"—through the images he provides of "insects, snakes and birds . . . in their own mystery, their own pristine being" (26).

But when Lawrence cites a passage to exemplify Crèvecoeur's presentation of "pristine being," what he actually cites is, interestingly, a passage dominated by a generalization that accords more closely with his own metaphysic than does the doctrine of Innocent Nature:

> "I am astonished to see," [Crèvecoeur] writes quite early in the *Letters,* "that nothing exists but what has its enemy, one species pursue and live upon the other: unfortunately our kingbirds are destroyers of those industrious insects [the bees]; but on the other hand, these birds preserve our fields from the depradations of crows, which they pursue on the wing with great vigilance and astonishing dexterity." (26)

Lawrence singles out, as representing "actual nature," Crèvecoeur's perception of conflict and contest in the natural world. But what the passage presents, of course, is as much an "idealization" as the concept of Innocent Nature. The idea of conflict informing this passage is a master concept in *Studies,* an idea governing Lawrence's model of the American psyche and of American literary texts: "the frictional opposition [of Americans] to the master they wish to undermine" (4), the opposition between conflicting impulses in the American psyche and that between the conflicting strata of meaning in American texts.

The conflict extends to Lawrence's own text: Lawrence cannot leave nature, in its "pristine being," alone. He very soon turns Crèvecoeur's kingbirds into allegorical figures:

> Crèvecoeur says he shot a king-bird that had been devouring his bees. He opened the craw and took out a vast number of bees, which little democrats, after they had lain a minute or two stunned, in the sun roused, revived, preened their wings and walked off debonair . . . like true Yanks escaped from the craw of the king-bird of Europe. I don't care whether it's true or not. I like the picture, and see in it a parable of the American resurrection. (27–28)

In writing of the kingbird, Lawrence allegorizes not only the American experience as he projects it but also his own critical enterprise in *Studies*: he "shoots down" the old, repressive "morality" wherever he finds it in the works he scrutinizes, opening their craws to release the stunned bees carrying the honey of passional "truth." Lawrence's citations from Crèvecoeur no more present the reader with the "pristine being" of the kingbird or with "actual nature" than his archaeological metaphor in *Apocalypse* offers a literal description of the text of Revelation.

To a certain extent, in *Apocalypse*, Lawrence merely substitutes "heathenish" Lawrentian allegory for the Christian allegorical interpretations of Revelation offered by his reviled predecessors. As Mara Kalnins has recently pointed out in her introduction to the Cambridge edition of *Apocalypse*, Lawrence reads Revelation as "an attempt to narrate a profound psychical experience in man, an experience too fundamental for rational explanation or scientific description" (4). Lawrence himself wrote of Saint John's Revelation: "It's a revelation of Initiation experience, and the clue is in the microcosm, in the human body itself . . ." (qtd. in Kalnins 4).

More than half of Lawrence's book (chapters X–XXII) attempts to excavate from the Christian overlay a pagan kernel or substratum of meaning, but as Lawrence systematically expounds the symbolism of the first half of Revelation—the seven seals, the cycle of the seven trumps, the woman clothed with the sun, the dragon, and the numerological symbols—he persistently assigns static meanings to symbols in a way that is difficult to distinguish from allegory—and he does so even at the moments where he is explicitly repudiating allegory. For example, he writes that

> The famous book of seven seals . . . is the body of man: of a man: of Adam: of any man: and the seven seals are the seven centres or gates of his dynamic consciousness. We are witnessing the opening, and conquest of the great psychic centres of the human body. The old Adam is going to be conquered, die, and be re-born as the new Adam: but in stages: in seven-fold stages: or in six stages, and then a climax, seven. For man has seven levels of awareness, deeper and higher: or seven spheres of consciousness. And one by one these must be conquered, transformed, transfigured.

> And what are these seven spheres of consciousness in a man? Answer as you please, any man can give his own answer. But in taking a common "popular" view, they are, shall we say, the four dynamic natures of man and the three "higher" natures. Symbols mean something: yet they mean something different to every man. Fix the meaning of a symbol, and you have fallen into the commonplace of allegory. (101)

It is extraordinary, the frequency with which Lawrence asserts the evil of fixing meaning as he is engaged in the very process of fixing meaning!

The recurrence of such passages throughout Lawrence's work suggests that the "fall" into allegory is an inevitability of critical discourse, an inevitability that Lawrence of course resisted with all resources available to him. Despite such resistance, however, one might argue that Lawrence's entire critical undertaking in *Apocalypse* is an allegory in the sense that he allegorizes the text of Revelation—much as he does the works he examines in *Studies*—as a battleground for competing moralities. He even writes in the "Introduction to *The Dragon of the Apocalypse* by Frederick Carter," which serves as a kind of introduction to *Apocalypse*, "Gradually we realize that the book has no one meaning. It has meanings. Not meaning *within* meaning: but rather, meaning against meaning" (48).

Another tacit admission that his writing in *Apocalypse* is contaminated by allegory is his use of a second critical procedure, one that does not assign meanings but rather attempts to communicate to modern readers "pagan consciousness," the kind of consciousness that would enable them to respond directly to the images of Revelation from "the deep emotional centres." But paradoxically, the more Lawrence tries to bring the modern reader "breast to breast with the cosmos"—as the pagan was—the thicker the barrier of abstraction, of language, he erects.

Lawrence attempts, for example, to instruct his readers in the methods by which pre-Christians read images or symbols. For the "modern process of progressive thought" (95)—"a movement in stages, like our sentences, and every full stop...a milestone that marks our 'progress' and arrival somewhere" (93)—the reader must learn to substitute "the old pagan process of rotary-image thought" where "Every image fulfills its own little circle of action and meaning, then is superseded by another image" (95). The process was intuitive and sensory, producing "a knowledge based not on words but on images. The abstraction was not into generalizations or into qualities, but into symbols. And the connection was not logical but emotional. The word 'therefore' did not exist" (91).

Lawrence exemplifies this nonlinear, nonverbal process by describing the magic workings upon the pagan mind of the riddle of the sphinx. He claims that "in the uncritical ancient who *felt* his images, there would spring up a great complex of emotions and fears" first in response to the perception of "animal difference and potency" evoked by the image of the thing that goes on four legs, then in response to the recognition of similarity—"as man realises himself an animal" (92). Such recognitions, Lawrence argues, occurred as "instant imaginative act[s], such as is very hard for us to achieve, but which children still make" (92). The vertical nature of these imaginative acts is stressed by Lawrence's use of the image of a whirlpool to convey ancient consciousness:

> To [the ancients] a thought was a completed state of feeling-awareness, a cumulative thing, a deepening thing, in which feeling deepened into feeling in consciousness till there was a sense of fulness. A completed thought was the plumbing of a depth, like a whirlpool, of emotional awareness, and at the depth of this whirlpool of emotion the resolve formed. But it was no stage in a journey. There was no logical chain to be dragged further. (93)

By avoiding the terminology of deliberate intellectual effort, Lawrence emphasizes the intuitive, nonverbal nature of the process he describes, but as a critical strategy the avoidance creates problems perhaps more obvious in his description of the reading of an ancient oracle. The enquirer, Lawrence explains, would ponder the "set of images or symbols of the real dynamic value [that is, the oracle], which [would] set the emotional consciousness . . . revolving more and more rapidly, till out of a state of an intense emotional absorption the resolve at last formed; or, as we say, the decision was arrived at" (93). The abstract, passive language that Lawrence uses here does little to bring the modern reader closer to the pre-Christian mind.

Indeed, it should be obvious that there is little that Lawrence can do in language—at least the language of critical discourse as opposed to art-speech—to foster in his readers intuitive or dynamic consciousness, the kind of consciousness he attributes to the pre-Christian mind. *Apocalypse* strongly suggests the futility of Lawrence's critical undertaking in that book—and of criticism in general. Any effort to explicate a text will necessarily involve some fixing of meaning, a kind of allegorization that is antithetical to the dynamic perception of meaning that Lawrence values in the process of reading. Criticism is of necessity conducted in language, which is linear and therefore discourages the kind of vertical and cyclical thought that characterizes dynamic consciousness.

Apocalypse does suggest, however, that though no single effort of explanation can successfully communicate the force of ancient symbols, we do possess the verbal resources to overcome some of the inherent limitations of criticism. If he cannot replicate in the modern mind "pagan consciousness," Lawrence can at least exercise his readers' minds in those alogical, vertical motions that constituted such consciousness, as for example through his use of repetition in the passage describing the ancient's encounter with *theoi*:

Everything was *theos*; but even so, not at the same moment. At the moment, whatever *struck* you was god. If it was a pool of water, the very watery pool might strike you; then that was god; or a faint vapour at evening rising might catch the imagination: then that was *theos*; or thirst might overcome you at the sight of the water: then the thirst itself was god; or you drank, and the delicious and indescribable slaking of thirst was the god; or you felt the sudden chill of the water as you touched it: and another god came into being, "the cold": and this was not a *quality*, it was an existing entity, almost a creature, certainly a *theos*: the cold; or again, on the dry lips something suddenly alighted: it was "the moist," and again a god. Even to the early scientists or philosophers, "the cold," "the moist," "the hot," "the dry" were things in themselves, realities, gods, *theoi*. And they *did things*. (95-96)

The passage presents us with a structure that duplicates in small the larger structure of portions of Lawrence's argument in which he returns again and again to the same idea, for example "pagan consciousness," through different examples; this passage attempts to set the mind revolving, revolving, about the concept of *theos* or god—attempts, that is, to duplicate in the reader's mind those movements Lawrence attributes to the "emotional mind" as he defines that term in his preface to Giovanni Verga's *Cavalleria Rusticana*:

...the emotional mind...is not logical....[It] makes curious swoops and circles. It touches the points of pain or interest, then sweeps away again in a cycle, coils round and again approaches the point of pain or interest. There is a curious spiral rhythm, and the mind approaches again and again the point of concern, repeats itself, goes back, destroys the time-sequence entirely, so that time ceases to exist, as the mind stoops to the quarry, then leaves it without striking, soars, hovers, turns, swoops, stoops again, still does not strike, yet nearer, nearer, reels away again, wheels off into the air, even forgets, quite forgets, yet again turns, bends, circles slowly, swoops and stoops again, until at last there is the closing-in, and the clutch of a decision or a resolve. (P 249-50)

The passage from *Apocalypse* leads the mind to make its curious swoops and circles around the concept of *theos,* each approach to the term having carried the reader through a different image or sensory term; but the passage has nowhere near the power of the passage from the review of Verga which verbally enacts the kinds of motions which it describes.

If the passage on *theos* succeeds to any degree in engendering in the reader a sense of emotional or intuitive, immediate understanding of the concept, that understanding is all the more noteworthy given the passage's remarkable summation of the predicament in which we live as language-making creatures. What the passage describes is a process of naming or, if you wish, a process of reading, interpreting, and reinscribing (in the mind) natural signs: "Everything was *theos*; but even so, not at the same moment." It was only when the pagan was *"struck"* by a natural object—or by a sensory perception—only when the pagan singled it out and conceptualized it as *theos,* that god came into being. If for the pagan these signs or concepts were "things in themselves, realities, gods, *theoi,*" they are nonetheless at least one remove from amorphous "everything": the dynamic source, the primal "complex activity of things existing and moving and having effect" which is the universe (52)—and which "is God" (95). It thus takes an act of separation and differentiation to make a "god" from "God." The separating power of language, which I would argue Lawrence sought to overcome through all his writing, is powerfully figured even by his model of primal connection with the gods.

The "Carbon" of Character: Two Models of the Self

The desire to connect with the world through language, the recognition that language disconnects us from the world: the tension between these two can be viewed as a tension between two different models of language.[3] One model, the symbolic model valorized by Lawrence's theory of art-speech, assumes that words have substance and that some necessary link exists between words and their signification, between signifier and signified. The other model, a differential model, recognizes the arbitrariness of the linguistic sign and assumes that "in language there are only differences *without positive terms*" (Saussure 120).[4] This differential model offers us language not as a system of signs uniting signifier and signified, but rather as a system of differences or differential relations among signifiers. A recognition of the differential nature of language informs the passage in *Apocalypse* where Lawrence describes the naming of the gods.

Lawrence's writing is informed not only by a tension between these two models of language but also by a tension between two corresponding models of the self. Associated with the symbolic model of language is an organic model of the self based upon the belief that the self is anterior to and independent of consciousness; a presence directly knowable by intuition (rather than indirectly knowable, through the mediating knowledge of something other),[5] the self is a center of personal identity of which all an individual says and does may be viewed as homogeneous expressions. According to the second model of the self, such a presence or center of personal identity is an illusion, an effect or product of differentiating relations with the other; the self is knowable only indirectly and inferentially, through knowledge of that which it is not.

These two models of the self are intertwined in the famous letter Lawrence wrote to Edward Garnett in June 1914, about a month after completing a draft of *The Rainbow*. The letter announces a break with traditional conceptions of character (and of the self). Expressing his interest in the Italian futurists, Lawrence writes that "that which is physic—non-human, in humanity, is more interesting to [him] than the old-fashioned human element—which causes one to conceive a character in a certain moral scheme and make him consistent" (CL II: 182).

In this letter, Lawrence rejects not only "the certain moral scheme" but also the demand for characters possessing the recognizable individuality that we associate with social realism, and he repudiates the traditional view of a character as a collection of traits that somehow reveal a center of personal identity or an essence. Rather than concerning himself with the ego or a conscious self that registers what we ordinarily call feelings, Lawrence prefers to see a character for what she *"is"*:

> I don't so much care what [a] woman *feels,* in the ordinary usage of the word. That presumes an *ego* to feel with. I only care about what the woman *is*—what she *is*—inhumanly, physiologically, materially—according to the use of the word: but for me, what she *is* as a phenomenon (or as representing some greater, inhuman will), instead of what she feels according to the human conception. (CL II: 183)

At the level of being that concerns Lawrence, the character may lack individualizing traits; her behavior is not necessarily explicable in psychological terms (for such terms reflect the "human conception" of self), nor does it necessarily refer the reader to some moral or spiritual center.

The new conception of character enunciated here, of course, poses many practical problems for the novelist;[6] but for our purpose it is most important to notice that Lawrence's "new" conception is based upon the same traditional model of the self as the "old-fashioned" conception that he rejects: despite his emphasis on the material, the physiological—the nonhuman—Lawrence is, in fact, introducing his own idea of essence here. He writes to Garnett:

> You mustn't look in my novel for the old stable ego of the character. There is another ego, according to whose action the individual is unrecognisable, and passes through, as it were, allotropic states which it needs a deeper sense than any we've been used to exercise, to discover are states of the same single radically unchanged element. (Like as diamond and coal are the same pure single element of carbon. The ordinary novel would trace the history of the diamond—but I say, "diamond what! This is carbon." And my diamond might be coal or soot, and my theme is carbon.) (CL II: 183)

According to Lawrence, a character in a traditional novel possesses a fixed core of identity, a stable center, to which all that the character says and does may be coherently referred. In reading novels, the reader is able to infer the presence of such a core, the presence of a unity or fixed center to the self, because the diverse actions of the character are selected and presented by the novelist—and understood by the reader—according to some such principle as moral or psychological consistency. Yet what does the metaphor of carbon allotropy do but introduce another such principle?

Difficult as Lawrence's novel may seem in its newness, his readers may learn to infer a unity, a "pure single element" of character, from the diversity of a character's actions. After all, to the scientifically trained mind, diamond and graphite are recognizable as different allotropes of carbon. Just so, to the reader who develops the "deeper sense" to which Lawrence refers, the allotropic states of character will presumably reveal themselves as "states of the same radically unchanged element." If readers succeed in discovering that element, they have discovered a principle of coherence or unity (never named by Lawrence) underlying the presentation of character; they have discovered an *essence*. That essence may not have the moral dimension or flavor that Lawrence associates with "old-fashioned" novels; that is, his characters may not conform to the "certain moral scheme" of traditional novelists. And the essential self of the Lawrentian character may be located in a different "place" (Lawrence implies that the other ego is "deeper" than the "stable ego" of traditional novels). But both conceptions presuppose the possibility of a homogeneous self, of a self all of whose manifestations are—theoretically, at least—unified by some principle of selfsameness.

The letter to Garnett also presses upon us a very different model of the self, one founded not on a principle of selfsameness or propriety but rather on a principle of difference. Lawrence's choice of carbon as a metaphor for the fundamental element of character is peculiar in that elemental carbon, like the other allotropic elements, is not really a "pure single element." It occurs in several different crystalline forms—its allotropes: diamond, graphite, and amorphous carbon (found in coal and soot). Thus it could be said that carbon is never purely or simply itself, for it always differs from itself, is always already something else also—diamond, graphite, amorphous carbon.

To put the case in this way is not to indulge in word games but rather to point out that in choosing carbon as a metaphor for the self-identity of character, Lawrence chooses a metaphor that troubles the very notion of self-identity. Carbon is not a single, self-identical material substance from which the allotropes are derived (as, we might say, a character in a traditional novel has a single, self-identical ego or core from which all the character's values and behavior are derived). Rather the notion of carbon as a "pure single element" derives from or is an effect of the differential relations among various items listed on the periodic table of the elements used by chemists and physicists. Like carbon, the pure single element of character or of the self is not a substance but a mental construct. The self is not known intuitively and directly any more than carbon is; rather it is known inferentially and indirectly, by means of its differential or differentiating relations with that which it is not.

This differential model of the self is more clearly implied in Lawrence's 1925 essay, "Art and Morality." In that essay, he argues that the function of art "is to reveal things in their different relationships" (P 524). Morality in art consists of fidelity to the way in which "we move with and amongst and against" (P 525) things in the universe. The presupposition of this theory is that "The universe is like Father Ocean, a stream of all things slowly moving. We move, and the rock of ages moves. And since we move and move for ever, in no discernible direction, there is no centre to the movement, to us. To us, the centre shifts at every moment" (P 525). Things have their being and identity not in isolation but in relation to each other. Because things are constantly shifting and moving and the relations among things constantly shift, there can be no center to the being of anything—or as Lawrence puts it—"the centre shifts at every moment." The essay implies a relational and differential model of the self: the self can exist or be defined only in relation to the not-self or the other, and as that which stands outside the self shifts, so must the self. The self can have no stable or fixed center.

"He who *triumphs,* perishes"

The differential models of the self and language are not so much deliberate conceptualizations as they are inescapable implications of Lawrence's rhetoric, rhetoric in the sense of "all the turnings of language away from straightforward referential meaning" (Miller, *Fiction and Repetition* 20). Taken together these models constitute a kind of metaphysic that tests or criticizes Lawrence's organic metaphysic (comprising the organic model of the self and the symbolic model of language). Lawrence writes of such "essential criticism" in the passage I have already quoted from "Study of Thomas Hardy":

> [E]very work of art adheres to some system of morality. But if it be really a work of art, it must contain the essential criticism on the morality to which it adheres. . . . The degree to which the system of morality, or the metaphysic, of any work of art is submitted to criticism within the work of art makes the lasting value and satisfaction of that work. (P 476)

In other words, no idea is ever "raised to a governing throne" in a work of art; any idea or ideal contained in that work is modified, qualified, or interrogated by other elements within the work.

It is probably no accident that the work that introduces the notion of "essential criticism," Lawrence's "Study of Thomas Hardy," also provides us with the first extended example of what that term might mean. The "essential criticism" provided by the relational and differential perspective seems to enter Lawrence's writing at roughly that point which Keith Cushman has called the "great watershed in Lawrence's career" (15): the point between *Sons and Lovers* and *The Rainbow.*[7] The break with traditional novelistic techniques, one might speculate, opened his prose to the fuller possibilities of figurative language—and, apparently as a consequence, to the differential metaphysic. Composed while he was at work on *The Rainbow,* Lawrence's "Study of Thomas Hardy" is not merely a work of literary criticism but also an ontological exploration that questions the ontology it embraces. That ontology centers on the concept of "excess," which serves as a kind of master concept in the study: "The excess is the thing in itself at its maximum of being" (P 404). The introduction of differential concepts in parts of the study raises, however, the question of whether we can properly speak of "the thing in itself" at all.

Lawrence's discussion, early in the text, of the process by which consciousness evolves suggests that entities have their being only through their difference from that which they are not. As Lawrence writes, an individual's consciousness is extended through knowledge of "the things that are not himself" (P 432): "I feel joy when I kiss, because it is not me, the kiss, but rather one of the bounds or limits where I end....[T]he kiss is a...division of me from the mass.... And the more that I am driven from admixture, the more I am singled out into utter individuality, the more this intrinsic me rejoices" (P 432).

The phrase, "intrinsic me," resists or evades the question of whether the "me" has being in isolation from the "not-me"; and within two pages of having introduced the possibility of a differential self, Lawrence in fact rejects the possibility:

> We start the wrong way round: thinking, by learning what we are not, to know what we as individuals are: whereas the whole of human consciousness contains, as we know, not a tithe of what *is,* and therefore it is hopeless to proceed by a method of elimination.... [W]e know that, in life, the new motion is not the resultant of the old, but something quite new, quite other, according to our perception. (P 434)

"Something quite new" is another name for "the excess," for creative fullness of being, but despite this reassertion of that master "theory of being" as overflowing presence, the differential possibility reasserts itself, in the next chapter but one, "Of Being and Not Being." In the sexual myth Lawrence creates there,

> no new thing has ever arisen...save out of the impulse of the male upon the female. The interaction of the male and female spirit begot the wheel.... As in my flower, the pistil, female, is the centre and swivel, the stamens, male, are close-clasping the hub, and the blossom is the great motion outwards into the unknown, so in a man's life, the female is the swivel and centre on which he turns closely producing his movement. (P 444)

Lawrence later claims that "the division into male and female is arbitrary, for the purpose of thought" (P 448); in other words, the division is figurative. One peculiarity of the long passage I have quoted is, then, the speed with which Lawrence grants his metaphors literal status or reference—and continues to do so:

> [I]deally, the soul of the woman possesses the soul of the man, procreates it and makes it big with new idea, motion, in the sexual act, yet, most commonly, it is not so. . . . Every man seeks in woman for that which is stable, eternal. And if, under his motion, this break down in her, in the particular woman, so that she be no axle for his hub, but be driven away from herself, then he must seek elsewhere for his stability, for his centre to himself. (P 445)

An irony here is that in shifting to the literal, as if under the compulsion to give his theoretic words concrete reference, Lawrence reintroduces the possibility that the self has no substantial being, that the only center the male has lies beyond himself: he must seek a "centre" in the other, in something beyond himself.

This possibility is confirmed and extended through the definition that Lawrence offers for "the religious effort of Man":

> The religious effort is to conceive, to symbolize that which the human soul, or the soul of the race, lacks, that which it is not, and which it requires, yearns for. . . . [I]t is the symbolizing of a great desire, the statement of the desire *in terms that have no meaning apart from the desire.* (P 447, emphasis added)

This admission that the Absolute, that God, is a mere projection of humanity's need for "that which is stable, eternal" (P 445) posits a glaring deficiency, a void, at the center of the self, indeed at the center of being. Lawrence describes the effects of that deficiency in vivid terms:

> Let a man walk alone on the face of the earth, and he feels himself like a loose speck blown at random. Let him have a woman to whom he belongs, and he will feel as if he had a wall to back up against; even though the woman be mentally a fool. No man can endure the sense of space, of chaos, on four sides of himself. It drives him mad. He must be able to put his back to the wall. And this wall is his woman.
>
> From her he has a sense of stability. She supplies him with the sense of Immutability, Permanence, Eternality. (P 446)

Since "woman" is but a *metaphor* here for a complement that has no objective existence, man's fear "that no woman can centralize his activity" (P 447) is always realized. The celebration of "the excess"—of creative fullness—in the Hardy study might thus be regarded as an effort to cover for a void at the heart of being that parts of the text uncover.

The alternation of two theories of being, being as presence and being as absence or difference, might well be emblematized by a passage from "The Crown" essays, Lawrence's next extended effort in the pollyanalytic mode: "There are the two eternities fighting the fight of Creation, the light projecting itself into darkness, the darkness enveloping herself within the embrace of light. And then there is the consummation of each in the other . . . which is absolute" (P II: 371). In "The Crown," which was composed shortly after

Lawrence completed *The Rainbow,* Lawrence's shifting from what Frederic Jameson calls "a substantive way of thinking to a relational one" (13) makes itself felt in the proliferation of relational terms that we find in it. It offers us, somewhat paradoxically, two infinites: "So that if there be universal, infinite darkness in the beginning, there must be universal, infinite light in the end. And these are two *relative halves*" (P II: 368, emphasis added); "Destruction and Creation are the two *relative absolutes* between the opposing infinities" (P II: 404, emphasis added); "God is the utter *relation* between the two eternities..." (P II: 410, emphasis added); the Holy Ghost is the "utter relation...timeless, absolute and perfect" (P II: 410); "Our souls are established upon all the timeless achieved relationships..." (P II: 412).

The first Crown essay, "The Lion and the Unicorn Were Fighting for the Crown," presents a theory of being which depends upon the concept of opposition or, to use Lawrence's term, "interopposition." The essay opens with a meditation upon the "strange and painful position" (P II: 365) of the two creatures: "to have for a *raison d'être* a purpose [triumphing over the other] which, if once fulfilled, would of necessity entail the cessation from existence of both opponents" (P II: 365). If the lion beats the unicorn, he does not win; he merely chases the unicorn out of town, erases or obliterates it; and, Lawrence asks, "Would not the lion at once expire, as if he had created a vacuum around himself?" (P II: 366). Lawrence explicitly presents the conflict between the lion and the unicorn as an emblem for the conditions under which humans have being: he argues that at "the core of our hearts" (P II: 366) is a void, a hollow want, an infant crying if the struggle is not engaged. Yet if this void is ever filled, if this need is ever satisfied, "there would be a great cessation of being, of the whole universe" (P II: 366)—"He who *triumphs,* perishes" (P II: 373). The "crown" over which the lion and the unicorn are fighting is a symbol of "the essential, intrinsic nature of God," which is conflict: "it is the fight of opposites which is holy" (P II: 374).

As William York Tindall has written, these essays make Lawrence's "enthusiasm clearer than what he had to say" (27), perhaps because Lawrence is now "[t]hinking more in terms of metaphors than principles" (Miko 207), "is more rapt" (Kermode 51), than in the Hardy study. So baffling are the transformations of the metaphors in "The Crown," at points, that one is tempted to read it as an allegory of nonreferentiality; that is, any attempt to read it referentially is repeatedly thwarted by Lawrence's shifting terms. The verbal difficulties posed by the essays may be related to the oppositional theory of being they present, a theory based upon a differential model of reality. As this study illustrates, Lawrentian oppositions frequently collapse.[8] For example, in the Hardy study, after constructing an elaborate argument on the basis of the opposition of stasis and motion, Lawrence dismantles that opposition by writing, "There is no such thing as rest. There is only infinite motion" (P 448). When Lawrence collapses a carefully constructed dichotomy in this way, it seems that it is the principle of *difference,* not the nature of the things that differ, that energizes his writing and shapes his thought.

The rest of this study will examine the ways in which this principle enters the novels surrounding the Hardy study and "The Crown," submitting the organic "metaphysic" or "morality" of these novels to criticism. Though Lawrence never relinquishes that metaphysic, his fictional masterpieces, *Sons and Lovers, The Rainbow,* and *Women in Love,* do represent an increasingly powerful questioning of the organic by the differential metaphysic.

2

Sons and Lovers:
A Metaphysical Unsettling

One point at which *Sons and Lovers* discloses its dominant metaphysic is the scene in which Paul Morel explains to Miriam Leivers why she likes one of his sketches so much: " 'It's because—it's because there is scarcely any shadow in it; it's more shimmery, as if I'd painted the shimmering protoplasm in the leaves and everywhere, and not the stiffness of the shape. That seems dead to me. Only this shimmeriness is the real living. The shape is a dead crust. The shimmer is inside really' " (152). The opposition between an outer dead crust and an inner vitality, between form and substance, presupposes the notion of essence; and Paul's speech grants value to immediacy, spontaneity, vitality— to temporal and spatial presentness. Direct presentation of the "shimmering" protoplasmic essence of things, were it possible, would be the artistic aim of Lawrence's youthful hero: it is not pine trunks at sunset that Paul paints in another picture, but " 'red coals, standing up pieces of fire,' " " 'God's burning bush...that burned not away' " (152).

The Flame of Immediacy

The values implied by Paul's speech are kept before the reader of *Sons and Lovers* through the pervasive imagery of light, warmth, and glowing color.[1] Walter Morel's "sensuous flame of life, that flowed off his flesh like the flame from a candle" (10), for example, appears to be an index to his full presence to himself and others; in the form of a ruddy glow, the flame permeates those scenes where he works happily at some domestic chore like mending boots: "he hammered the soft, red-glowing stuff on his iron goose, and made the shape he wanted. Or he sat absorbed for a moment, soldering. Then the children watched with joy as the metal sank suddenly molten, and was shoved against the nose of the soldering-iron, while the room was full of a scent of burnt resin and hot tin, and Morel was silent and intent for a moment" (63).

The powerful association that part I forges between fire imagery and the "real living" quality in Morel, the vividness and warmth that inspire such joy in his children, is especially well exemplified by the admirable passage describing Morel's breakfast routine:

> He went downstairs in his shirt and then struggled into his pit-trousers, which were left on the hearth to warm all night. There was always a fire, because Mrs. Morel raked. And the first sound in the house was the bang, bang of the poker against the raker, as Morel smashed the remainder of the coal to make the kettle, which was filled and left on the hob, finally boil. His cup and knife and fork, all he wanted except just the food, was laid ready on the table on a newspaper. Then he got his breakfast, made the tea, packed the bottom of the doors with rugs to shut out the draught, piled a big fire, and sat down to an hour of joy. He toasted his bacon on a fork and caught the drops of fat on his bread; then he put the rasher on his thick slice of bread, and cut off chunks with a clasp-knife, poured his tea into his saucer, and was happy. (27)

Morel's activities center about the fire, which seems to illumine each object he uses, each action he performs, in turn. As in the passage where Morel mends his boots, "joy" is a focal word, the confluence of streams of sensory, emotional, and mental details—or to use Lawrence's own words from his definition of "the art-symbol or art term"—of the "emotional and passional, spiritual and perceptional, all at once" (qtd. in Armin 40). The term "joy" scarcely registers itself as abstract because of the way in which the passage bolsters it with the fond delineation of specific detail. We might in fact expect Mr. Morel to sit down to an hour of toast and tea; when he sits down to "an hour of joy," our delight derives from the unexpected precision of the abstract phrase. And by virtue of its position at the end of a sequence of parallel phrases presenting specific actions and concrete objects, the phrase "was happy" assumes some of the substance and radiance of the objects themselves.

Part I of *Sons and Lovers* presents us with analogous passages in which the mother's presence makes itself powerfully felt as she engages in domestic tasks that center about the fire:

> She liked to do things for [William]: she liked to put a cup for his tea and to iron his collars, of which he was so proud. It was a joy to her to have him proud of his collars. There was no laundry. So she used to rub away at them with her little convex iron, to polish them, till they shone from the sheer pressure of her arm. (55)

> She spat on the iron, and a little ball of spit bounded, raced off the dark, glossy surface. Then, kneeling, she rubbed the iron on the sack lining of the hearth-rug, vigorously. She was warm in the ruddy firelight. Paul loved the way she crouched and put her head on one side. (66)

As in the passage describing Mr. Morel's breakfast routine, the concrete seems to absorb the abstract, and the abstract seems to absorb the concrete. Emotive terms like "love" and "joy" have the force of sensory detail, and concrete terms have the force of symbol. The shine produced by Mrs. Morel's proud labor, her warmth in the ruddy firelight—these are physical and emotional at once.

The coalescence of concrete and abstract in such passages might be viewed as the stylistic correlative of presence. The pervasive imagery of heat and light in such passages constitutes an index to the value of the immediate, full emotional presence of the parents. Lawrence is not, however, investing a particular emotion like love with value; rather he is privileging an emotional intensity that betokens immediacy. The value of such intensity becomes plain in an episode like the one in which Mr. Morel shears William's baby curls:

> Mrs. Morel lay listening, one Sunday morning, to the chatter of the father and child downstairs. Then she dozed off. When she came downstairs, a great fire glowed in the grate, the room was hot, the breakfast was roughly laid, and seated in his arm-chair, against the chimney-piece, sat Morel, rather timid; and standing between his legs, the child—cropped like a sheep, with such an odd round poll—looking wondering at her; and on a newspaper spread out upon the hearthrug, a myriad of crescent-shaped curls, like the petals of a marigold scattered in the reddening firelight. (15)

The episode presents a violation of Mrs. Morel in which the child is shorn of the mother's influence, the "myriad of crescent-shaped curls, like the petals of a marigold scattered in the reddening firelight"; *her* child, "cropped like a sheep," is a sacrifice to the father's need to assert himself, to affirm his masculinity by making sure nobody mistakes *his* boy for a "wench." The great fire, the excessive heat, the reddening firelight all intimate the emotional conflagration to follow: "[Mrs. Morel] gripped her two fists, lifted them, and came forward. Morel shrank back. 'I could kill you, I could!' she said. She choked with rage, her two fists uplifted" (15). The light in the scene operates as a kind of textual spotlight, drawing our attention to the scene's significance. Mrs. Morel "remembered *the scene* all her life, as one in which she had suffered *the most intensely*" (16, emphasis added).

In these and many other passages in *Sons and Lovers,* especially in part I, the coalescence of sensory detail and emotional import, of concrete and abstract, further endorses the values communicated through the imagery of heat and light: the values of immediacy, spontaneity, and presence. Now it is important to recognize that this stylistic trait corresponds to a belief in the symbolic nature of language: a belief in the possibility of a seamless unity of language and truth, image and idea, signifier and signified. Such a belief appears to animate those earnest, "struggling, abstract speeches" of the adolescent Paul Morel. But when he talks to Miriam about his painting, he does so in a context where the light imagery makes significant counterstatements to the implications of his speech.

Ultimately the scene, which I quote at length, suggests a problematic relation between language and reality, especially reality defined as the "real living":

[T]he girl gradually sought him out. If he brought up his sketch-book, it was she who pondered longest over the last picture. Then she would look up at him. Suddenly, her dark eyes alight like water that shakes with a stream of gold in the dark, she would ask:
"Why do I like this so?"
Always something in his breast shrank from these close, intimate, dazzled looks of hers.
"Why *do* you?" he asked.
"I don't know. It seems so true."
"It's because—it's because there is scarcely any shadow in it; it's more shimmery, as if I'd painted the shimmering protoplasm in the leaves and everywhere, and not the stiffness of the shape. That seems dead to me. Only this shimmeriness is the real living. The shape is a dead crust. The shimmer is inside really."
And she, with her little finger in her mouth, would ponder these sayings. They gave her a feeling of life again, and vivified things which had meant nothing to her. She managed to find some meaning in his struggling, abstract speeches. And they were the medium through which she came distinctly at her beloved objects. (152)

The passage constitutes an implicit claim that Paul apprehends things directly—intuitively and immediately; he sees into the heart of things, the passage seems to argue, while Miriam is scarcely capable of seeing what is right in front of her eyes: she needs Paul's "struggling, abstract speeches" to clarify her world for her and to enable her to come "distinctly at her beloved objects."

But *does* Miriam need to be enlightened by Paul's speeches? The imagery of light associated with her eyes creates a peculiar ambiguity which unsettles the narrative's implicit claims, an ambiguity as to the source of light in the scene, the location of the fire. Do her "dark eyes alight like water that shakes with a stream of gold" merely reflect the shimmer in the painting she scrutinizes or are they lighted from within, giving Paul (and us) a glimpse of the "shimmering protoplasm" of her being? Are her "dazzled looks" a sign of the fire within or of her staring too fixedly at a fire without (Paul or his painting)? Where is "the real living"—the vital presence—signified by the imagery of light? The possibility "that Miriam represents the 'shimmeriness' that is 'the real living'" (Schwarz 264) would seem to counter the claim that she needs Paul's speeches to give her "a feeling of life."

But the text says that they "gave her a feeling of life *again*" (emphasis added). The curious qualification added by *again* opens two possibilities. It may be that the "feeling of life" reflected in Miriam's eyes can only be hers through mediation. She needs Paul's words not only to grasp the world, but also to come into contact with herself, to apprehend the flame of life within her or to have that flame "kindled." Or it may be that Paul's speeches actually deaden Miriam's initial lively intuitive response to the painting (she ponders his words dumbly with "her little finger in her mouth"). Then it would be by her own reanimating of the dead husks of his pronouncements—in other words, by her own imaginative effort—that things which had meant nothing to her are revivified or given meaning ("She managed to find some meaning in his struggling, abstract speeches").

The text does not enable us to decide between these two possibilities, but in the case of the second possibility it is worth noticing that Miriam would end up doing what the passage claims Paul does for her: vivifying things that had "meant" nothing to her. And she would end up doing so in spite of the obstacle that Paul's words (abstract meanings) had posed for her. The passage can be said to differ with itself not only in this suggestion but also in Paul's shrinking from Miriam's "close, intimate, dazzled looks," an action that contradicts the values implied by his speech, values endorsed by much of the imagery of the novel. In art, the "real living" essence is what Paul wishes to uncover, but in life, apparently, too close an approach to the "protoplasm," the "inside," is a threat. Because he feels threatened, Paul's speech is actually a duplicity: it is a response to Miriam that attempts to evade her, to distract him from her disturbing presence.

In its ambivalence as a verbal gesture, Paul's speech encompasses a dichotomy that characterizes the representation of verbal intercourse throughout the novel. On the one hand, the verbal relations of the characters in the novel suggest the power of language to create meaning and unity: the power of language for communication and communion. On the other hand, they also dramatize the ways in which language can be used to subvert communication and prevent intimacy.

Narrative Evasion and the Exile from Presence

The text urges us to believe, for example, in the power of speech to create a sense of "real living" in the Morel family. The Morel children depend upon talk with their mother: "Nothing had really taken place in them until it was told to their mother" (62). In turn, Mrs. Morel depends upon talk with her children, especially Paul, for her sense of having a "real" life. Each evening after returning from work at Jordan's, Paul tells her the events of his day: "His life-story, like an Arabian Nights, was told night after night to his mother. It was almost as if it were here own life" (113). And Mrs. Morel secures her tie to Paul through talk: "She waited for his coming home in the evening, and then she unburdened herself of all she had pondered, or of all that had occurred to her during the day. He sat and listened with his earnestness. The two shared lives" (114). Mrs. Morel and her children create a common reality through talk.

In part II of *Sons and Lovers,* sexual metaphors urge the reader to believe in the fecundity of speech between Paul and Miriam. Paul takes "the most intense pleasure in talking about his work to Miriam. All his passion, all his wild blood, went into this intercourse with her, when he talked and conceived his work. She brought forth to him his imaginations. She did not understand, any more than a woman understands when she conceives a child in her womb. But this was life for her and for him" (202). Miriam not only stimulates Paul's imagination but also leads him to fuller consciousness, to understanding of his intuitions: "He was conscious only when stimulated. A sketch finished, he always wanted to take it to Miriam. Then he was stimulated into knowledge of the work he had produced unconsciously. In contact with Miriam he gained insight; his vision went deeper" (158).

These passages seem to attribute to Miriam a role similar to that attributed to Paul in the passage where we learn that his "struggling, abstract speeches," his "sayings," give Miriam "a feeling of life" and vivify "things which had meant nothing to her." But the suggestion that Paul's speeches beget her vision of the world ultimately subverts our sense of a mutually sustaining or "fertilizing," creative interdependency between the two adolescents. An obvious irony in their intercourse is that it is utterly chaste for much of the novel. In shaping Miriam's vision of the world, Paul also urges her toward a particular view of herself, one dictated by his own psychological requirements. A clinical view of those requirements is likely to conclude that Paul needs Miriam to remain nonsexual, virginal.[2] His efforts to protect her virginity account for Paul's use of speech to avoid communication and to prevent intimacy.

Lawrence uses nonhuman, almost brutal metaphors to characterize some of Paul's unacknowledged efforts to put words between himself and the ripening Miriam: "Miriam was the threshing-floor on which he threshed out all his beliefs. While he trampled his ideas upon her soul, the truth came out for him. She alone was his threshing floor. She alone helped him towards realization" (227). Miriam has good reason for feeling "as if he were using her unconsciously as a man uses his tools at some work he is bent on" (228), but despite appearances to the contrary, the pursuit of truth is not Paul's work here. Rather it is the evasion of intimacy on which he is "bent."

One never learns much about the religious conflict that Paul is supposed to be suffering, or if or how he resolves it; but one easily recognizes that Paul's discomfort as he reads from the Bible has a sexual, not an intellectual, cause: "he began to falter and get self-conscious. And when he came to the verse, 'A woman, when she is in travail, hath sorrow because her hour is come,' he missed it out. Miriam had felt him growing uncomfortable. She shrank when the well-known words did not follow" (228). Paul's omission hints that his Bible reading and expounding are calculated to put a distance between him and Miriam—or to distract him from the sexual possibilities thrust upon him by her appearance in this scene: "She wore a large white hat with some pinkish flowers. It was a cheap hat, but he liked it. Her face beneath was still and pensive, golden-brown and ruddy" (227–28). She is virginal but tempting.

Paul's most characteristic strategy for avoiding intimacy is not, however, to discuss religion, but rather to make pronouncements about Miriam's personality and feelings. In this respect, at least, *Sons and Lovers* seems accurately to reflect Lawrence's relationship with Jessie Chambers, who writes in *D. H. Lawrence: A Personal Record,* about Lawrence's tendency to "label" her:

> He declared I was like Emily Bronte, which I resented, feeling it was a false short-cut to understanding me, like sticking a label on. To all my protests he merely shook his head. (130)

> Finally he told me I had no sense of humour, and it occurred to me that if it were so I should be too angry to listen to him. . . . I could only reveal myself to him by what I was, and his crude groping into the recesses of my personality confused me and made me shut up tight. (132)

> Lawrence had found a new name for me. I was no longer Emily Bronte. I was a pre-Raphaelite woman. I disliked the new label even more than the old one. It made me feel that for him I was becoming less and less of a suffering, struggling human being, and more and more of a mental concept, a pure abstraction. (145)

Paul Morel, of course, labels Miriam, tells her who or what she is, sometimes in terms approximating those mentioned by Jessie Chambers. Paul's claim that Miriam "'is never jolly, or even just all right'" (152) corresponds, for example, to Lawrence's claim that Jessie Chambers "had no sense of humour." But furthermore Paul's attempts to give names to Miriam's personality traits and feelings follow a pattern that resembles the one adumbrated in *D. H. Lawrence: A Personal Record*: Paul makes an assertion about Miriam; if she replies, she denies the assertion; Paul then reaffirms his initial statement; even if Miriam has previously attempted to argue, she may now "shut up tight"—be quieted by chagrin, confusion, or frustration; if she should attempt to argue again, Paul changes the subject.

The following interchange between Paul and Miriam illustrates both the pattern to which I am referring and its oedipal motivation:

> "I wish you could laugh at me just for one minute—just for one minute. I feel as if it would set something free."
> "But"—and she looked up at him with eyes frightened and struggling—"I do laugh at you—I *do*."
> "Never! There's always a kind of intensity. When you laugh I could always cry; it seems as if it shows up your suffering. Oh, you make me knit the brows of my very soul and cogitate."
> Slowly she shook her head despairingly.
> "I'm sure I don't want to," she said.
> "I'm so damned spiritual with *you* always!" he cried.
> She remained silent, thinking, "Then why don't you be otherwise." But he saw her crouching, brooding figure, and it seemed to tear him in two.
> "But there, it's autumn," he said, "and everybody feels like a disembodied spirit then." (188)

Paul's need to be so spiritual with Miriam may partly be explained by noting that "her crouching, brooding" presence recalls a vivid image of his mother that Paul registered as a child: "kneeling, she rubbed the iron on the sack lining of the hearth-rug vigorously. She was warm in the ruddy firelight. Paul loved the way she crouched and put her head on one side" (66). In the later scene Miriam crouches in the firelight: "she crouched on the hearth-rug near his feet. The glow was warm on her handsome, pensive face as she kneeled there like a devotee" (186). The parallels in imagery of course provoke the idea that Miriam reanimates one of Paul's revered images of his mother. Whether such a reanimation would lead him to identify Miriam with his mother or to be reminded of his primary loyalty to Mrs. Morel, Miriam's crouching on the hearth likely insists upon the young woman's untouchability for him. Yet he blames Miriam for his being "so damned spiritual with [her] always."

The coincidence of images suggests the possibility of another reawakening in Paul of childhood memories. In the firelight, his mother made his heart "contract with love": "When she was quiet, so, she looked brave and rich with life, but as if she had been done out of her rights" (66). In the later scene Paul may feel torn in two because he knows that in a sense Miriam is being done out of her rights. He has devoted his talk, earlier in this scene, to the subject of Clara Dawes, commenting on "'her mouth—made for passion—and the very setback of her throat'" and pointedly admiring "'her skin and the texture of her—and . . . a sort of fierceness somewhere in her'" (187). No wonder if there is some suffering in Miriam's laughter here. Paul has avoided intimacy with her by anatomizing Clara's sensual charms.

Miriam's silent challenge of Paul's judgment of her here—that she is humorless or too serious and too spiritual—provokes from him an evasive generalization as response. The pattern repeats itself a few scenes later, where he becomes so intense discussing Michelangelo that "his voice gradually filled her with fear, so level it was, almost inhuman, as if in a trance" (194). Paul rejects Miriam's attempts to curtail his speech, insisting to her that his talk is what her "unconscious self" really wants from him no matter what her conscious self may say. He continues in "his dead fashion": "'If only you could want *me*, and not what I can reel off for you!'" (194). To Miriam's bitter contradiction—"'I! Why, when would you let me take you?'"—Paul replies with an insincere gesture of defeat: "'Then it's my fault,' he said, and, gathering himself together, he got up and began to talk trivialities" (194).

Such a scene repudiates Paul's notion that Miriam wants "to draw all of him into her" (194), that belief being a reflection of his mother's fear that Miriam "'is one of those who will want to suck a man's soul out till he has none of his own left'" (160). [3] Rather than encouraging Paul's spiritual intensity, his baring of his soul, Miriam tells him to be quiet, to save himself. How remarkable are the deadness and automatism with which he persists in his notions about Miriam, and then his willingness to give up his pursuit of truth as soon as she threatens, with her questions, to spoil his illusions about her! One could of course cite scenes in which Paul is more overtly manipulative and even abusive. In discussing the scenes in which Paul "condescends" to teach Miriam, for example, Kate Millett has written that the passages represent "some of the most remarkable instances of sexual sadism disguised as masculine pedagogy which literature affords until Ionesco's memorable *Lesson*" (253). But even more disquieting than Paul's verbal behavior in scenes like those I have discussed and those to which Millett refers is that the pattern of manipulative and ultimately destructive verbal behavior represented by those scenes not only governs Paul's conversations with Miriam but also more subtly seems to direct the narrative procedure of those sections of part II that focus on Paul's relationship with Miriam. The specific pattern is this: the narrator makes certain assertions about Miriam; Miriam's dramatized behavior may constitute an implicit challenge to those assertions, but narrative commentary of a reductive sort repeatedly reasserts the thesislike statements about Miriam's character or personality. Miriam, like Jessie Chambers, tends to "shut up tight," and her actions are frequently ambiguous. Consequently, by the end of the novel, the narrator's assertions about her may well hold sway in the reader's mind *even though the text provides evidence enough for a counterinterpretation of her character.*[4]

The narrator presents his major assertions about Miriam's personality in the lengthy "description" of her that occurs at the beginning of part II:

> The girl was romantic in her soul. Everywhere was a Walter Scott heroine being loved by men with helmets or with plumes in their caps. She herself was something of a princess turned into a swine-girl in her own imagination. And she was afraid lest this boy, who, nevertheless, looked something like a Walter Scott hero, who could paint and speak French, and knew what algebra meant, and who went by train to Nottingham everyday, might consider her simply as the swine-girl, unable to perceive the princess beneath; so she held aloof.
>
> Her great companion was her mother. They were both brown-eyed, and inclined to be mystical, such women as treasure religion inside them, breathe it in their nostrils, and see the whole of life in the mist thereof. So to Miriam, Christ and God made one great figure, which she loved tremblingly and passionately when a tremendous sunset burned out the western sky, and Ediths, and Lucys, and Rowenas, Brian de Bois Guilberts, Rob Roys, and Guy Mannerings, rustled the sunny leaves in the morning, or sat in her bedroom aloft, alone, when it snowed. That was life to her. For the rest she drudged in the house, which work she would not have minded had not her clean red floor been mucked up immediately by the trampling farm boots of her brothers. She madly wanted her little brother of four to let her swathe him and stifle him in her love; she went to church reverently, with bowed head, and quivered in anguish from the vulgarity of the other choir-girls and from the common-sounding voice of the curate; she fought with her brothers, whom she considered brutal louts; and she held not her father in too high esteem because he did not carry any mystical ideals cherished in his heart, but only wanted to have as easy a time as he could, and his meals when he was ready for them. (142-43)

As Gavriel Ben-Ephraim has written, "The commentary is deft, but we should be wary of it—its tone is a bit too confident, its revelations too categorical. Lawrence employs the absolutes he disbelieved in when he portrays the farm-girl whose life is all make-believe and idealization..." (90). The passage anticipates a number of assertions about Miriam that are made more pointedly and negatively later in the text: she is overly religious, overly romantic, and overly sensitive; discontent with her lot and not completely in touch with reality, she has an abnormal craving for affection but is unable to get along with others.

When we state the implications of the passage this bluntly, it is easier to see that, as Louis L. Martz has shown, the view of Miriam presented by the narrator at the opening of part II finds *substantiation* only through the obviously blurred vision of Paul (Martz 348–51). Before this passage, Miriam appears in the novel only once, in the episode where Paul visits Willey Farm with his mother. The attention there to the girl's ruddiness—to her "rosy dark face," her "beautiful warm colouring" (124–25)—suggests that she, like Walter Morel, embodies "the dusky, golden softness" of the "sensuous flame of life" (10). Furthermore, her effort in that introductory episode to overcome her fear of feeding chickens directly from her hand surely suggests that life is really more to her than the trembling passion with which she supposedly indulges in her romantic daydreams: Miriam would like to be considered more "ordinary" than others consider her, more normal. She is not necessarily "something of a princess turned into a swine-girl in her own imagination"; quite possibly she is something of a swine-girl turned into a princess by the imaginations of others—her mother, her brothers, and Paul.

Nothing in the text really *dramatizes* the excessive religiosity imputed to Miriam. She goes to chapel regularly, as does Paul. She has a picture of Saint Catherine on her bedroom wall, a picture she admires for its dreamy quality. On at least one occasion she wears a rosary that Paul has given her; on another, at age sixteen, she falls to her knees in frightened prayer when she realizes that she loves Paul.

These indications of an inclination toward mysticism in Miriam are far outweighed by abundant evidence of mysticism in Paul. He is first attracted to the Leivers family by the mother's religious intensity: "Everything had a religious and intensified meaning when he was with her. His soul, hurt, highly developed, sought her as if for nourishment" (148). Mrs. Leivers's way of exalting "everything—even a bit of housework—to the plane of a religious trust" (146) exerts a "subtle fascination" on him and in effect levels the distinctions he sees when he is with his mother, who is "logical" (147). Much later in Paul's relationship with Miriam, she finds occasion to be frightened by his mysticism. After first making love with Miriam, Paul lapses from ordinary consciousness into a state where "life seemed a shadow," where "night, and death, and stillness, and inaction ... seemed like *being*. ... The highest of all was to melt out into the darkness and sway there, identified with the great Being" (287).

Some critics have taken Miriam's horror at the mystic in Paul here as a sign of her supposed sexual repression, but Daniel A. Weiss convincingly argues that Paul's desire to lose individuality through sexual intercourse implies a need for "the ultimate regression to the child's status with its mother": "It is Miriam's refusal to allow him to regress to the Nirvana, the paradisal state of the infant, her insistence that he recognize her, that fills him with anguish" (53) and accounts for his breaking off their relationship. It is thus a projection when Paul attributes the torment and ultimate failure of their sexual relationship to Miriam's spirituality; he "spiritualizes" their sexual relationship to satisfy his own psychological needs.

It is not merely by means of narrative commentary that the narrator endorses or recommends Paul's view. The organization and narrative procedure of some sections of part II subtly but illegitimately insist upon the truth of certain undramatized generalizations about Miriam. The portion of the narrative treating Paul's relationship with Mrs. Leivers illustrates this point. The focus on relationship between Paul and Miriam's mother soon broadens to include Miriam, and to identify the girl with her mother— "Miriam was her mother's daughter" (148). But the drama that follows only partly justifies the identification.

The scene in which Paul and the two women discover a jenny wren's nest illustrates a cycle of creative interaction that characterizes his early relationship with both mother and daughter: both apparently stimulate him into opening his eyes to his surroundings, which he then sketches in words or water colors, thus bringing the object of representation into clearer focus or fuller being for his companions. The pattern is confirmed by a second brief episode in which Paul, accompanied by Miriam, notices some "celandines, scalloped splashes of gold, on the side of the ditch" (148). After Paul explains to Miriam what he likes about the flowers, the narrator makes the following remarks:

> And then the celandines ever after drew her with a little spell. Anthropomorphic as she was, she stimulated him into appreciating things thus, and then they lived for her. She seemed to need things kindling in her imagination or in her soul before she felt she had them. And she was cut off from ordinary life by her religious intensity which made the world for her either a nunnery garden or a paradise, where sin and knowledge were not, or else an ugly, cruel thing.
>
> So it was in this atmosphere of subtle intimacy, this meeting in their common feeling for something in Nature, that their love started. (148)

In general, before closing with its hazy generality about their common love for nature, the narrative unit moves from an emphasis on the nourishment that

Paul receives from Mrs. Leivers to a greater emphasis on the nourishment that Miriam receives from Paul—from the "spell" that the mother casts on Paul to the "spell" that Paul casts on the daughter.

This movement is characteristic of the presentation of Miriam throughout in that any *exposure* of Paul's needs is usually balanced or outweighed by *analysis* of Miriam's. The summation—"she stimulated him into appreciating things thus, and then they lived for her"—seems irreproachable since the pattern has been dramatized twice in swiftly succeeding scenes. Yet why the apparently irrelevant insistence that Miriam is anthropomorphic? Nothing that precedes this sentence indicates how she is anthropomorphic (and in fact it is slightly unclear whether she stimulates Paul *because* she is anthropomorphic or *even though* she is). Paul, one might argue, has taken an *anthropomorphic* view of the flowers in observing that they seem " 'to be pressing themselves at the sun' " (148), but applied to Miriam the term seems a label designed to certify in advance Paul's accusations that Miriam is always wheedling the soul out of things, begging them to love her (218)—in other words, that she wants to possess things and to possess them on her own limited, personal terms. But this view is most likely dictated by Paul's attachment to his mother (Martz 353). So is much else in the paragraph that I have quoted.

If Miriam needs "things kindling in her imagination or in her soul" before she feels she "has" them, so does Paul, as the next paragraph but one reveals: "But Mrs. Leivers and her children were almost his disciples. They kindled him and made him glow to his work, whereas his mother's influence was to make him determined, patient, dogged, unwearied" (149). Perfectly characteristic of the narrator's "shiftiness" in this section of the novel is the way in which similar conditions or needs in Paul and in Miriam are presented in terms of an opposition; the emphasis on Miriam's passive need as a contrast to Paul's inspired activity subtly prepares the way for one of Paul's cruelest accusations: " 'You aren't positive, you're negative. You absorb, absorb... because you've got a shortage somewhere' " (218). Again, Mrs. Morel's view.

What I have called the narrator's shiftiness also emerges in the way in which action trails off into summation which, in turn, shades off into commentary only superficially related to the preceding drama. The transitions in the paragraph that presents Miriam as anthropomorphic, needy, excessively religious, hypersensitive and alienated ("And then... and then... And she was....") may create the effect that facts are being related in terms of causality; but actually they are a clue to the looseness of the connections that the paragraph proposes. The narrator here mimes Paul's verbal behavior by piling assertion upon assertion, each one less concretely objectified than the preceding one and therefore insisted upon all the more strongly; when the narrator turns from the subject of Miriam's isolation in her "religious intensity" to conclude, "So it was in this atmosphere of subtle intimacy, this meeting in their common feeling for something in Nature, that their love started" (148), what we hear is something like the voice of Paul: the Paul who, torn in two by Miriam's brooding presence, trails lamely off, " 'But, there, it's autumn...and everybody feels like a disembodied spirit then' "(188). Yet it is very important to recognize that because narrative commentary of the sort I have been analyzing here *precedes* those conversations where Paul most blatantly fails to respond to Miriam's timid confrontations, his failures, when they do occur, are the less noticeable: they do not necessarily seem failures at all because they repeat a pattern of discourse familiar to the reader from exposure to ostensibly reliable narrative.

The narrative may in other ways deflect the reader's attention from an alternate picture of Miriam that emerges from the action. There is, for example, the abruptness with which the narrator, who can change the subject as fast as Paul can, shifts scenes. A sequence from "Lad-and-Girl Love" will illustrate this point. In one scene Miriam shows Paul a swing in the cow shed. Fascinated by the spectacle of his swinging, she is still frightened when he swings her. The sexual yearning that lies beneath Miriam's fear becomes pronounced when she watches Paul swing one more time and realizes that she "could never lose herself so.... It roused a warmth in her. It were almost as if he were a flame that had lit a warmth in her whilst he swung in the middle air" (151).

At this point, in a manner that merely mimes a genuine transition, the narrator abruptly shifts the focus from Miriam's incipient sexuality to Paul's intimacy with the rest of the family: "And gradually the intimacy... concentrated for Paul on three persons—the mother, Edgar, and Miriam.... [T]o Miriam he more or less condescended, because she seemed so humble" (151–52). The next scene, the one in which Paul makes his "struggling, abstract speech" about the "shimmeriness" of the painting that she admires, seems calculated to illustrate Miriam's humility, the inferiority of her perceptions, and her consequent willingness to defer to Paul's opinion. But the exposure of the "real living" quality in Miriam, through the light imagery in the passage, may account for the fact that the next scene comes across almost as a revision of the preceding one, as a new version designed to insist more effectively on Miriam's liabilities.

There Paul preaches to Miriam about another of his paintings—and about herself: she is " 'never jolly, or even just all right' "; she is " 'different inside,' " not " 'ordinary' " (152–53). While Paul argues, he finds that Miriam gets "so near him" that he experiences "a strange roused sensation" (153). The emotional logic of the rather abrupt transition to the next scene—"Then sometimes he hated her" (153)—is clear; the words present a fair summary of

Paul's reaction to any situation where he begins to respond sexually to Miriam. Yet the reader may not fully apprehend the logic, for the scene introduced by these words attempts to forward the idea that Miriam has an abnormal craving for love. When she kneels and folds her little brother in her arms, she provokes Paul to "suffering because of her extreme emotion": "Her intensity, which would leave no emotion on a normal plane, irritated the youth into a frenzy" (153).

It is of course ironic that Paul should become frenzied because of her intensity, but the text acknowledges the irony of his overreaction only by a sudden shift to commentary about the lack of flexibility and life in Miriam's body. It is as if the narrator realizes that he has revealed Paul's fear of the intensity and openness of Miriam's emotions and attempts to cover—or at least compensate for—the exposure by changing the subject. But in so doing, the narrator contradicts the judgment implied by the scene he has left behind. There Paul wishes that Miriam possessed "his mother's reserve" (153); here she is subtly indicted because "[t]here was no looseness or abandon about her" (154). The scene that "illustrates" Miriam's restraint shows Paul teaching her to overcome her fear of jumping over stiles. Yet she learns relatively easily while Paul is "frightened" not only by "a kind of ecstasy" that blazes in her eyes as they run down the fields, but also by the "wild 'Ah!' of pain" with which she precedes her safe landing on the other side of the stile. Once again the scene shifts, this time to one introduced by the words "She was very much dissatisfied with her lot" (154). The narrator revives the princess-turned-swine-girl thesis.

Thus the narrative both does and does not allow the action to reveal character. Scene after scene presents evidence of Paul's limitations and Miriam's potentialities, but shifts in the focus of the narrative are conducted in such a way that they may prevent the reader from assimilating and judging the evidence, evidence that contradicts the narrator's *assertions* about Miriam.[5] Such a failure is especially likely since the lengthy dissection of Miriam's character which appears at the beginning of part II may predispose the reader to accept Paul's view of Miriam. That predisposition may in turn continually be reinforced by narrative commentary of a reductive, simplifying sort: "He was now about twenty-three years old, and, though still virgin, the sex instinct that Miriam had over-refined for so long now grew particularly strong" (252). One might call this the view of a self-deceived neurotic couched in the language of an objective, authoritative onlooker who has access to all the facts.

By means of this pose of authority the narrator of *Sons and Lovers* attempts to shape the reader's view of Miriam much as Paul, in his conversations with her, attempts to shape her view of herself. The view proposed is that Miriam is passive and nonsexual—undesiring and undesirable. In closing his eyes to Miriam's sensuous appeal and embracing this view of her, Paul forfeits "the glow," "the shimmer," the "real living" quality in her. To the extent that Miriam allows herself to assent to this view, she allows herself to be victimized by Paul. And to the extent that readers allow this view to command their unquestioning assent, they allow themselves to be victimized by the narrator of *Sons and Lovers.*

The narrative procedures I have scrutinized here may be viewed as constituting a psychological "game" of the sort that contemporary psychologists have categorized and anatomatized, a game of the sort in which we find only three basic game roles: victim, persecutor, and rescuer (Steiner 181–85). One might argue that critics of *Sons and Lovers* have played all three roles. The most prominent of the "persecutors" is Mark Schorer, whose response to the narrative difficulties of the novel is not merely the claim (in his famous essay, "Technique as Discovery") that Lawrence failed to master the past through "technique," but also a more general judgment that is telling in its harshness: "The handling of the girl, Miriam, if viewed closely, is pathetic in what it signifies for Lawrence, both as man and artist."[6]

Other critics have attempted to "rescue" the novel from such charges by giving the problems Schorer saw names like "technique" and "form." One such rescuer, Louis L. Martz, argues that ambiguities and contradictions in the presentation of Miriam constitute a successful "technique" for rendering the ambivalence of the protagonist (351). Though Martz is surely correct in much of his carefully detailed treatment of Miriam, one must question his smooth way of disposing of the novel's presentation of that character by claiming that "it works" (351). After all, for many perspicacious readers who have accepted the narrator's view as accurate and objective—Keith Sagar, Dorothy Van Ghent, Mark Spilka, and even at times Kate Millett—that presentation does not "work" in the way Martz means: it does not succeed in reflecting the patterns of the hero's distorted consciousness.[7]

In a more recent essay than Martz's, Daniel R. Schwarz has argued that "the discrepancies between the narrator's interpretations and ours create a tension that becomes an intrinsic part of the novel's form" (255). To justify this view, Schwarz must emphasize the value of the reader's participation "in the agonizing but wonderfully exciting *aesthetic* process by which an author tries to give shape and unity to his recent past" (255). But *Sons and Lovers* does not really invite the kind of participation that Schwarz mentions; the text in many ways—for example through the narrator's pose of authority—discourages and frustrates any such participation as well as readers' attempts to counterpoise their own interpretations to the narrator's.

A striking feature of the articles by Martz and Schwarz is the poor fit between their highly insightful analyses of detail and their dubious generalizations, a problem that curiously duplicates the narrative split that is a central concern here. The difficulty seems to arise in these two articles—as does Schorer's almost moralizing judgment of *Sons and Lovers*—from viewing the novel in formalistic terms. The formalistic demand for unity or organic wholeness may lead critics, on the one hand, to make harsh, moralizing judgments about a book that they may on many grounds love to read and teach; or it may tempt them, on the other hand, to smooth over the jagged edges of Lawrence's treatment of the past, in the process stretching notions of form and technique beyond recognition in an effort to make them fit the often recalcitrant facts of the novel.

If, as Calvin Bedient has suggested, the "burgeoning of psychology into metaphysics is the hidden drama of *Sons and Lovers*" (118),[8] then a more just appreciation of the novel may arise from suspending formalistic preconceptions about fiction and viewing the novel in epistemological terms. From such a perspective, the text may be seen as one in which the point of view reflects a belief in the possibility of truth and in the power of language to uncover the truth; at the same time, however, the narrative "facts" presented in the text undermine those beliefs. That is, the story the narrator undertakes to tell deconstructs the belief in an unambiguous relation between language and truth. Like Paul's story, the narrator's quest for truth dramatizes an exile from a world of clarity, immediacy, and presence to one of obscurity, deferment, and absence.

Sacrifice as Derelict Signifier

One way of charting this exile is by examining the journey of the word *sacrifice* through the text, for it is through this linguistic journey that the text erodes the belief in the unity of signifier and signified. Although the sacrifices of Mrs. Morel are lovingly delineated in part I, the word *sacrifice* itself occurs only twice—in the scene where Paul sacrifices Arabella, Annie's doll (57–58). In this episode, the word *sacrifice* refers to the burning of an object that Paul hates seemingly "because he had broken it." One might draw an analogy between Paul's feeling in this episode and the hatred he later feels for Miriam, whom he also "breaks" in the sense of damaging her emotionally as well as in the sense of taking her virginity. The analogy is worth keeping in mind in examining part II, where the term *sacrifice* rings out again and again, always in connection with Miriam but never quite definite in its referent.

Initially, the narrator employs the term to establish Miriam's need to sacrifice herself to love, but the use of the term is shadowed by dubieties. At sixteen, overwhelmed by her feelings for Paul, Miriam prays not to love Paul but almost immediately notices an anomaly in her prayer:

How could it be wrong to love him? Love was God's gift. And yet it caused her shame. That was because of him, Paul Morel. But, then, it was not his affair, it was her own, between herself and God. She was to be a sacrifice. But it was God's sacrifice, not Paul Morel's or her own. . . . [S]he fell into that rapture of self-sacrifice, identifying herself with a God who was sacrificed, which gives to so many human souls their deepest bliss. (171-72)

The sense in which Miriam is to be a sacrifice is unclear: she may be thinking in terms of loss of virginity (though it is unlikely she can formulate that fear at this point), or she may be thinking of the diversion of some of her love from God to Paul. Furthermore, it is ambiguous in what sense love causes Miriam shame *because of Paul.* Is she ashamed to love him as opposed to someone else, or is she aware of the shame he projects upon her? In either case, her adolescent, idealistic confusion of human and divine love is like that experienced by Ursula Brangwen in *The Rainbow,* who outgrows it.

The generality of the language—"the rapture of self-sacrifice . . . which gives so many human souls their deepest bliss"—should alert the reader to the presence of that narrator who identifies closely with the neurotic, speechifying Paul, the Paul who argues, expounds, insensitively labels Miriam, and misconstrues his own experience. But though we never again see Miriam "identifying herself with a God who was sacrificed," the passage's suggestion that Miriam needs to make of herself a sacrificial victim is one which the narrative repeatedly attempts to reinforce through its use of *sacrifice.*

For example, as the notion of sacrifice expands to include actual suffering that Miriam experiences in her relation with Paul, the narrative nonetheless insinuates that Miriam likes to suffer: "She did not at the bottom believe she would ever have him. . . . Certainly she never saw herself living through a lifetime with him. She saw tragedy, sorrow, and sacrifice ahead. And in sacrifice she was proud, in renunciation she was strong, for she did not trust herself to support everyday life" (215). Either Miriam will be a sacrifice in that Paul will reject her and her devotion to him will have been wasted; or she will sacrifice herself to remaining with a lover who, as she says elsewhere, constantly fights her off.

More disquieting than the inexact referent of the term *sacrifice* here is that the strength in renunciation and pride in self-sacrifice attributed to Miriam are actually *dramatized* not by her behavior but by Paul's. He glories in sacrificing himself to his mother's love: "And he came back to [his mother]. And in his soul was a feeling of the satisfaction in self-sacrifice because he was faithful to her. She loved him first; he loved her first" (222). Furthermore, he "sacrifices" himself in connection with Miriam, as we see in one scene where he finds it impossible to kiss her passionately:

[Miriam] felt she could bear anything for him; she would suffer for him. She put her hand on his knee as he leaned forward in his chair. He took it and kissed it; but it hurt to do so. He felt he was putting himself aside. He sat there sacrificed to her purity, which felt more like nullity. How could he kiss her passionately when it would drive her away, and leave nothing but pain? Yet slowly he drew her to him and kissed her. (282)

"He sat there sacrificed to her purity": the language here disguises the agent of the sacrifice, who is, of course, Paul himself. Miriam is suffering for him in this scene because "[h]is eyes [are] dark with torture" (281-82) and she is "sorry for him" (281). And it is not that his kiss drives her away but rather that her passion seems to extinguish his. Miriam is "fascinated" by "a peculiar dark blaze" in Paul's eyes when she kisses him, but when she "look[s] into his eyes with her full gaze of love," "[t]he blaze struggle[s], seem[s] to try to get away from her, and then [is] quenched. It was a moment of anguish" (282). Paul sacrifices himself here, and not to Miriam's purity but to his requirement that she remain pure.

There is abundant evidence that despite her Victorian upbringing, Miriam does not equate sex with sacrifice (as Louis L. Martz's essay on *Sons and Lovers* amply documents), yet there is an ironic sense in which Miriam is a sacrifice: for in refusing to acknowledge her evolving identity in all of their passionate exchanges, Paul sacrifices her individuality to his need for that deathlike state which Weiss has described as "the ultimate regression to the child's status with its mother" (53). Miriam's awareness of this sacrifice accounts, as we have seen, for her horror the first time they make love: "He seemed to be almost unaware of her as a person: she was only to him then a woman. . . . She relinquished herself to him, but it was a sacrifice in which she felt something of horror. This thick-voiced, oblivious man was a stranger to her" (286). It is in this scene, through sex, that Paul discovers that the "highest of all was to melt out into the darkness and sway there, identified with the great Being" (287). At the same time, however, he is disturbed that Miriam "had not been with him all the time" (286). The irony is, of course, that he has no more "been with" her than she has been with him.

The use of the term *sacrifice* is so hedged with local ambiguities and dubieties that larger ironies do not immediately present themselves to the reader. Let us look, for example, at the scene where Paul and Miriam make love at Miriam's grandmother's cottage, a scene where we see Paul disemburden himself of his consciousness of Miriam as a desiring individual by attributing to her a sacrificial attitude. Part of the narrative easily accommodates this view. As Paul approaches the bed,

her hands lifted with a little pleading movement, and he looked at her face, and stopped. Her big brown eyes were watching him, still and resigned and loving; she lay *as if* she had given herself up to sacrifice: there was her body for him; but the look at the back of her eyes, *like* a creature awaiting immolation, arrested him, and all his blood fell back" (289-90, emphasis added).

The passage clearly indicates that Paul sees Miriam as a kind of sacrifice; it makes no attempt to tell us how she feels.

A later passage, however, is not so clear in its attribution of thoughts and feelings: "She was very quiet, very calm. She only realised she was doing something for him. He could hardly bear it" (290). In the first sentence, "quiet" describes Miriam literally; "calm" may or may not represent her state. The second sentence seems to make a statement about her frame of mind, but since the third gives Paul's feeling about that state of mind, we begin to wonder if the second, too, merely represents his viewpoint.

Similar remarks might be made about the next four sentences: "She lay to be sacrificed for him because she loved him so much. And he had to sacrifice her. For a second, he wished he were sexless or dead. Then he shut his eyes again to her, and his blood beat back again" (290). Once more the passage opens with a sentence that might be taken as a direct statement about Miriam's feelings, but subsequent sentences lead the reader to wonder if the entire passage does not represent Paul's point of view. Such narrative ambiguities shunt to one side a crucial sacrifice indicated by the words "he shut his eyes again to her."

A cold shadow falls over the narrative in this episode at the point when Paul approaches Miriam in bed; prior to this point the language of the episode recalls the glow of Paul's childhood in its loving handling of domestic details:

> Miriam was busy preparing the dinner.... The sunlight came through the leaves of the scented geraniums in the window. She was cooking a chicken in his honour. It was their cottage for the day, and they were man and wife. He beat the eggs for her and peeled the potatoes. He thought she gave a feeling of home almost like his mother, and no one could look more beautiful, with her tumbled curls, when she was flushed from the fire. (288)

Later, as they walk out into the field, Miriam's face is "all overcast with a golden shine": " 'like a transfiguration,' " Paul says (289). Miriam agrees with Paul that it is a "great day" and the narrator tells us, "She *was* happy, and he saw it." The light imagery again functions as the correlative of Miriam's happiness, communicating the almost palpable presence of her joy. The departure from the narrative of the glow is an analogue to Paul's shutting of his eyes to Miriam's desire.

The narrative projection of Paul's fears upon Miriam also characterizes the scene where Paul and Miriam part for the last time. After Mrs. Morel's death, Miriam offers to marry Paul, who rejects the offer. While stating that Miriam "could easily sacrifice herself," the text is contradictory in its suggestions about the sense in which this is true. On the one hand, Miriam would be sacrificing herself if she married Paul because she wants him but he does not want her very much. On the other hand, the text also insinuates, however illegitimately, that Miriam still views sex as sacrifice; consequently, marriage to a person who wanted her would constitute a sacrifice.

Other dubieties surround the use of the term *sacrifice* here, not only ambiguities as to point of view like those we have already encountered in earlier scenes, but outright contradictions: "[Miriam] felt that now he lay at her mercy.... [She] dared not put her arms around [his body].... She was afraid he would not let her" (417). Such narrative confusions compete for attention with Paul's desire to sacrifice himself, to relinquish himself to some warm, possessive embrace that relieves him of self-responsibility.

An emphatic assertion of Miriam's rapture in self-sacrifice immediately precedes the admission that Paul wishes to abdicate self-responsibility:

> She turned her face aside; then, raising herself with dignity, she took his head to her bosom, and rocked him softly. She was not to have him, then! So she could comfort him. She put her fingers through his hair. For her, the anguished sweetness of self-sacrifice. For him, the hate and misery of another failure. He could not bear it—that breast which was warm and cradled him without taking the burden of him. So much he wanted to rest on her that the feint of rest only tortured him. He drew away. (418)

The pattern, in which Miriam's putative motives are allowed to overshadow Paul's, recurs in the next narrative paragraph:

> It was the end then between them. She could not take him and relieve him of the responsibility of himself. She could only sacrifice herself to him—sacrifice herself every day, gladly. And that he did not want. He wanted her to hold him and say, with joy and authority: "Stop all this restlessness and beating against death. You are mine for a mate." She had not the strength. Or was it a mate she wanted? or did she want a Christ in him? (418)

Again the nature of Miriam's sacrifice is indeterminate. She does, after all, want to marry Paul, and the idea that she sees sex as sacrifice has been made dubious by the preceding narrative. Yet those curiously disjointed questions which conclude the paragraph attempt to insinuate that idea. The resulting confusion may prevent the reader from asking the more relevant question here: Does Paul still want a Mary in Miriam? His desire for a mate is couched in terms that call to mind the embrace of his mother; earlier, when his relationship with Miriam seems to be draining him of joy, Mrs. Morel feels herself fighting "against his . . . will to die" and is heartbroken by his "poignant carelessness about himself" (258). Paul still seeks someone who will care for him the way his mother did.

The scene contradicts itself yet once again: "He felt, in leaving her, he was defrauding her of life. But he knew that, in staying, stifling the inner, desperate man, he was denying his own life. And he did not hope to give life to her by denying his own" (418). No longer rejecting Miriam because she will not "take the burden of him," he here rejects her because he does not wish thus to give his life away. If this is to represent a sudden shift to a greater sense of self-responsibility, gained through suffering, Lawrence scarcely gives the reader a chance to register Paul's courage and growth, for the narrative shifts abruptly again to Miriam: "She suddenly looked at him. Her bitterness came surging up. Her sacrifice, then, was useless" (418). *Sacrifice* here suggests Miriam's sacrifice of pride in offering herself to Paul, the waste of her love, or the loss of her virginity, but the intensity of the language in this episode and the insistent repetition of the term *sacrifice* urge us to seek sacrifices more fully circumstantiated by the text at the same that it obscures such sacrifices.

The shifts of meaning and point of view in this scene might be viewed as producing the kind of "unique tension" to which Louis L. Martz refers (351), one that reflects the agony of the moment, but they also prevent the narrative from ever focusing on the strength of either of the characters. The scene never quite acknowledges Miriam's growth in the novel, nor her dramatized potential for growth, nor Paul's courage in giving her up. Nor does the use of term *sacrifice,* so central to this scene and others, ever quite enable the reader to focus, at least with ease and clarity, on the most profound sacrifice dramatized by the novel: Paul's failure to see Miriam clearly, which entails for him a sacrifice of vision and of self-realization and for Miriam that withering of response that is her way of dealing with his manipulations. Rather, the term is employed so often and with such a range of problematic and contradictory suggestion that in the final pages of the novel, where its repetition is most emphatic, its referent or referents seem further in the distance from the reader than at any other point in the text.

Darkness and the Reality of Difference

The automatism of the narrator's repetitions of the term *sacrifice* thus constitutes an evasive strategy resembling that familiar to us from Paul's speeches: the repetitions create the effect of meaning or communication at the same time that they prevent it. Louis L. Martz has commented that once the narrative turns to the relations of Paul and Clara, "everything comes back into clarity and firmness" (364); Paul's experiences with Clara result in a higher degree of self-knowledge in him and, Martz argues, "a consequent clarity and precision in the remarks of the narrator" (366). But the narrator's continued focus on self-sacrificial gestures or images—images of Clara kneeling and crouching—suggests that the narrator projects Paul's needs and feelings upon Clara as well as upon Miriam, thus continuing to blur the boundaries between Paul and his lovers. When, for example, Clara visits Baxter Dawes in the hospital, the narrator focuses upon her self-sacrificial attitude:

> The meeting was not a success. But she left him roses and fruit and money. She wanted to make restitution. It was not that she loved him.... Only she wanted to humble herself to him, to kneel before him. She wanted now to be self-sacrificial. After all, she had failed to make Morel really love her. She was morally frightened. She wanted to do penance. She kneeled to Dawes, and it gave him a subtle pleasure. (383-84)

This would make more sense as a fantasy of Paul's than as an actual occurrence. Very little if any of Clara's dramatized behavior prepares us for this scene, which comes across as a direct response to Paul's accusations that she mistreated Baxter—and now mistreats Paul. Clara's impulse to make restitution is finally significant in the Freudian scheme of the novel, where Paul's impulse to return her to Baxter is a way of "closing . . . the parental arch over his head again—an arch that in his own real family is crumbling" and restoring "the mother [i.e., Clara] to her former purity" (Weiss 33, 37). By symbolically recreating his family through returning Clara to Baxter, Paul becomes "the idealized son, who through suffering and sacrifice has achieved knowledge and power, the attributes of messiah-hood, an acceptance through expiation" (Weiss 34). Paul's strong motive of self-sacrifice then would account for the narrator's projection of that motive upon Clara.

Thus if the last four chapters of *Sons and Lovers* are not characterized by the sorts of distortion that accompany the presentation of Miriam, they still by no means constitute a return to the clarity of part I. The glow seems permanently to have disappeared from the novel. Paul's relationship with Clara is conducted in darkness, and even where the novel presents their daytime activities, the imagery rarely suggests the presence of light. For example, the dominant image of the long scene where they make love by the Trent River is "red clay"—an image singularly lacking in "shimmer," radiance, or luminosity.

Images of darkness characterize their relationship because its primary value for them is that it enables them to lose individuality in a sort of experience that offers no sharp outlines, no beloved objects, no distinctive qualities to be illuminated. Indeed, the great scenes of sexual passion in *Sons and Lovers* reverse the imagistic values of the novel, allying being as presence with darkness rather than with light. We have already seen that with Miriam Paul discovers that "night, and death, and stillness, and inaction . . . seemed like *being*. To be alive, to be urgent and insistent—that was *not-to-be*" (287). Now with Clara:

> They felt small, half-afraid, childish and wondering, like Adam and Eve when they lost their innocence and realised the magnificence of the power which drove them out of Paradise and across the great night and the great day of humanity. It was for each of them an initiation and a satisfaction. To know their own nothingness, to know the tremendous living flood which carried them always, gave them rest within themselves. If so great a magnificent power could overwhelm them, identify them altogether with itself, so that they knew they were only grains in the tremendous heave that lifted every grass blade its little height, and every tree, and living thing, then why fret about themselves? They could let themselves be carried by life, and they felt a sort of peace in each other. There was a verification which they had had together. Nothing could nullify it, nothing could take it away; it was almost their belief in life. (353–54)

Despite their reversal of the dominant imagistic values of the novel, these passages by no means dislocate the underlying metaphysic of *Sons and Lovers*, the novel's privileging of being as presence. Paul and Clara experience their nothingness figuratively, that is, only in relation to the immensity of the presence of "the tremendous living flood which carried them always." They come to know, through each other, what mystics know: if they are "only grains in the tremendous heave," the tremendous heave of the universe is nonetheless contained within the grains; the "magnificent power [that] could overwhelm them, [can] identify them altogether with itself."

The "verification," the "confirmation," that Paul and Clara receive through this "baptism of life, each through the other" (361) does not, however, guarantee the continued possibility of union. We read of Clara:

> It was almost as if she had gained *herself*, and stood now distinct and complete. She had received her confirmation; but she never believed that her life belonged to Paul Morel, nor his to her. They would separate in the end, and the rest of her life would be an ache after him. (361)

The passage curiously echoes the one in which Miriam is said never to have believed at bottom that she would have Paul: "Certainly she never saw herself living happily through a lifetime with him. She saw tragedy, sorrow, and sacrifice ahead" (215). Both passages indicate an awareness of Paul's inability to mate himself with anyone. The parallels between the two passages, however, argue against our merely locating that awareness in the consciousness of each of Paul's lovers and urge us rather to think of that awareness as another instance of narrative displacement of Paul's feelings to Miriam and Clara. In such displacement or projection, Paul's lovers come to stand in relation to Paul as signifier to signified; and Paul's failed relation with each of these women might be seen as another means by which the novel dramatizes the disjunction of signifier and signified.

The self, "distinct and complete," that Clara acquires through her relation with Paul is contaminated with a longing that implies a sense of incompletion: "the rest of her life would be an ache after him." This longing, one presumes, would refer her forever to Paul so that she could not in any meaningful sense be said to have a self "distinct and complete." Likewise Paul's echoings of his mother's view of things, especially his echoing of her view of Miriam, "refer" him constantly to her, so that he might be said to stand as signifier to her (transcendental) signified. From this point of view, the conclusion of *Sons and Lovers* yields interesting perceptions regarding Lawrence's drama of the sign:

> Everywhere the vastness and terror of the immense night which is roused and stirred for a brief while by the day, but which returns, and will remain at last eternal, holding everything

in its silence and its living gloom. There was no Time, only Space. Who could say his mother had lived and did not live? She had been in one place, and was in another; that was all. And his soul could not leave her wherever she was. Now she was gone abroad into the night, and he was with her still. They were together. But yet there was his body, his chest, that leaned against the stile, his hands on the wooden bar. They seemed something. Where was he?— one tiny upright speck of flesh, less than an ear of wheat lost in the field. He could not bear it. On every side the immense dark silence seemed pressing him, so tiny a spark, into extinction, and yet, almost nothing, he could not be extinct. Night, in which everything was lost, went reaching out, beyond stars and sun. Stars and sun, a few bright grains, went spinning round for terror, and holding each other in embrace, there in a darkness that outpassed them all, and left them tiny and daunted. So much, and himself, infinitesimal, at the core a nothingness, and yet not nothing.

"Mother!" he whispered "mother!"

She was the only thing that held him up, himself, amid all this. And she was gone, intermingled herself. He wanted her to touch him, have him alongside with her.

But no, he would not give in. Turning sharply he walked towards the city's gold phosphorescence. His fists were shut, his mouth set fast. He would not take that direction, to the darkness, to follow her. He walked towards the faintly humming, glowing town, quickly. (420)

The imagery here clearly recalls that in the great love scene between Paul and Clara, but here the immensity of the night is terrifying for it signifies absence, not presence. Paul's perception that there was "only Space" constitutes the novel's ultimate acknowledgment of the reality of difference, deferment, spacing. Paul is "at the core a nothingness" because he has his being only in relation to his mother, whom "his soul [cannot] leave," and "she was gone abroad." Yet he is "not nothing," for "there was his body, his chest, that leaned against the stile." When Paul turns "sharply towards the city's gold phosphorescence," he chooses presence, an ideal the contamination of which by negativity, by difference, is reflected in the false glow of the "gold phosphorescence" of the town.

3

The Rainbow:
The Resistance to Difference

The Rainbow is an anomaly among Lawrence's novels in that the characters simply do not talk very much. Those scenes that have commanded the deepest sympathy of readers give the effect of being conducted in silence: Tom's proposal to Lydia, his vigil with Anna in the barn, Anna and Will's stacking of the sheaves, their visit to Lincoln Cathedral, Anna's solitary dance in front of her bedroom fire, Ursula and Skrebensky's intercourse beneath the moon—in these scenes speech occurs, but as an intrusion calling characters back to selves of less grandeur than those suggested by their movements or by Lawrence's rendering of their subjective states.[1] The implication that some region of inarticulate interchange is the ground of being for the characters is not, of course, peculiar to this novel, for we find it at points throughout Lawrence's writing. What is peculiar is the degree to which the novel sets verbal activity at nought when the opening pages so clearly place high value on "utterance" as a means of fulfillment for the characters. This peculiarity is but one manifestation of the text's resistance to the differential metaphysic that nonetheless makes itself powerfully felt in the novel.

Two Models of Language in *The Rainbow*

The opening pages of the novel establish a dualistic framework in which the horizontal land on which the Brangwens labor is opposed to the vertical church tower that looms above and beyond them in the distance. The men, who are turned "*inwards* to the teeming life of creation" (3, emphasis added), stand in opposition to the women, who face *outwards* from the farm, looking "out to the road and the village with church and Hall and the world beyond" (3). And counterpoised to "the intercourse between heaven and earth," "the heated blind intercourse of farm-life" (2), is the verbal intercourse that constitutes experience in the world beyond. The Brangwen women have for generations "looked out from the heated blind intercourse of farm-life to the spoken world beyond. They were aware of the lips and the mind of the world speaking and giving utterance, they heard the sound in the distance, and they strained to listen" (2–3). The metaphors of speech stress the speechlessness, the wordlessness, of life at Marsh Farm; and it would seem that it is *because* their lives are circumscribed by inarticulate men that the Brangwen women yearn towards "the spoken world beyond," the world of verbal articulation. "It is," Lawrence writes in his contemporaneous work, "Study of Thomas Hardy" (1914), "a disproportion, or a dissatisfaction, which makes [a person] struggle into articulation" (P 460).[2]

Like the rest of the novel, the opening pages are pervaded with an ambivalence toward language and culture.[3] The evocation of "the intercourse between heaven and earth" has much more powerfully captured the sympathies of readers than has the description of the world of verbal intercourse, "the spoken world beyond." But if the Brangwen men derive a pseudosense of wholeness from their silent, "blind intercourse" with nature, their mothers and wives are at least subliminally aware of the fragmentariness to which they are all consigned in their isolation.

The ambivalence is encompassed by antithetical meanings of the term *articulate,* a word that assumes considerable importance in the novel as its repetitions imply a way of measuring succeeding Brangwen generations against one another. (Tom Brangwen is "inarticulate" [14, 100]; Will is "half-articulate" [108, 109]; if anyone is fully articulate in the novel, it is the well-educated Ursula, although the term is never used in connection with her.) Embracing the ambivalent possibilities of *jointing*—joining and dividing— the term *articulate* is divided against itself in the sense that it signifies, on the one hand, unity and coherence (to express in coherent verbal form, to unite by means of a joint) and, on the other hand, segmentation and separation (consisting of segments united by joints, distinctly marked off, formulated in clearly distinguished parts).

If the Brangwen quest for wholeness is intimately linked to an increasing degree of articulateness, as the women's yearning toward the spoken world beyond implies, then that wholeness, like the ideal state of *balance* of which Lawrence writes in his study of Hardy, is "never to be found" (P 447). It is an ideal, an abstraction, an imagined or "symbolized" state of being, the yearning for which stirs the characters to struggle *outward* toward "the beyond" or the "further [fuller] life." Wholeness is, in short, knowable only by its *difference* from, its *absence* from, the actuality experienced by the Brangwens.

This is the implication even of the opening chapter of the novel, which is literally split by difference in that it is the only chapter Lawrence has divided into two parts (I and II). The Ur-Brangwens introduced in part I inhabit a primal world in which they are united with nature yet divided from "the spoken world beyond," and the presentation of their almost Edenic existence within the ancestral enclave is laced with the terminology of difference. The Brangwens' farm lies "in the meadows where the Erewash twisted sluggishly through alder trees, *separating* Derbyshire from Nottinghamshire," and though comfortably fixed, the Brangwens "never become rich because there were always children, and the patrimony was *divided* every time" (1, emphasis added).[4] The first thing that we learn about the women is that they were "different" (2) from the men. And we later learn that the men "defer" (13) to the women in the house. *To defer,* of course, can mean to create a temporal difference by postponing or, as is the case in Lawrence's text, to acknowledge a kind of moral or spiritual difference by submitting to another's authority. Lawrence's use of "different" and "defer" embraces the possibilities signified by *différance,* Jacques Derrida's term for the "lag inherent in any signifying act," a term that underscores the semantic relation of *differ* and *defer.*[5]

We should not underestimate Lawrence's sensitivity to double or multiple meanings, nor should we ignore the force of punning in his text.[6] Witness the skill with which he counterpoints the two different senses of "surety" associated with the Brangwens: the male *expectancy* signaled by his "look of an inheritor" (1) and the female *self-assurance* as she moves about in the house "with surety" (2). The men and women are the same, in possessing "surety," and yet different. Much more important is the sexual punning, near the beginning of the novel, which links the linguistic and the sexual. We read that the farm women view the life of the Lady of the Hall as an "epic," "their own Odyssey," a "poem" the "male part" of which "was filled in by such men as the vicar and Lord William . . . " (5). The puns occurring in the description of the male role in the poem strengthen the implication of the textual and linguistic metaphors: that we should read the sexual difference thus underscored in metalinguistic terms, that is, in terms of what the relations between the men and women may disclose about language.

From this point of view, the Brangwen women stand in relation to the Brangwen men as the spoken world stands in relation to the women. Just as the women live "in" Mrs. Hardy of the Hall, so do the men live "in" what is rather awkwardly called "the woman": "The woman was the symbol for that further life which comprised religion and love and morality. The men placed in her hands their own conscience. . . . [T]he men rested implicitly in her" (13). If the men, referring "their own conscience" to "the woman"—placing it in her hands—"rest implicitly in her," then we might say that their conscience is implied by her, and she becomes the signifier of their moral being. But in thus displacing their conscience, the men in a sense empty their moral significance into "the woman." Thus she becomes truly a symbol, a term that partakes of the reality it signifies.

This view of their relations, however, is complicated by a second. When the text asserts that the men look toward the women as symbols of "that further life" or of "higher being," the opposition between the inert, inward-facing men and the highly motivated, outward-facing women breaks down, for the men duplicate the activity of women who look outwards for symbols of "a higher form of being" than blood intimacy offers them.[7] All the Brangwens, in some sense or another, may be seen as "fighting outwards toward knowledge" (3).[8] By dismantling the hierarchical opposition between the men and the women, the text opens itself to a second conception of language or the linguistic sign. At the same time that she is to the Brangwen men the symbol of "the further life," the woman herself displaces her own significance upon "the spoken world beyond." She *refers* herself to that world; and life, fullness of being—her own unrealized potential—are signified to her by the activities of the inhabitants of that world, signifiers that spin themselves like "the endless web" of the Odyssey. If the men locate their meaning or significance in the woman, and the woman locates her meaning or significance in the world beyond, and the world beyond is presented as a system of signs, then the relations of the Brangwens to each other and to the world constitute a system of deferral and substitution that resembles the structure of language conceived as a system of differences or differential relations among signifiers.

Thus the relations of the Brangwen men and woman mirror two alternate theories of the linguistic sign, one in which the sign is viewed as a unity of signifier and signified (the symbolic conception of the sign) and one in which the sign is viewed as a signifier that has its significance in its relation to other signifiers (the differential conception of the sign). As the rest of this chapter demonstrates, *The Rainbow* sets up considerable resistance to the differential conception of the sign (and of language and of reality). One indication of that resistance is that use of "the woman" to refer to many Brangwen wives and mothers, a usage that coincides with the text's disclosure of the way in which "the woman" differs from herself. Though she represents both the symbolic and differential conceptions, Lawrence privileges the former conception through his use of a term positing unity.

Indifference and Literalization as Reactions to Difference

The novel's resistance to the differential model of language more obviously emerges through the relations of Anna Brangwen and then of her daughter Ursula to the Word. For both, verbal formulation, at least of religious feelings or "truths," elicits merely a painful sense of absence, of the disparity between words and their referents. Although the rosary she inherits from her father fills Anna with a "strange passion" (99) and the "mystic words" (100) of the Latin church service inspire her love, she detects "a discrepancy, a falsehood" (100) when the words are translated. As long as religious terms and symbols have only indefinite referents for Anna, they retain their power over her; but with understanding comes the inevitable reduction of the richly evocative symbol to a mere sign:

> [S]he was moved by 'benedictus fructus ventris tui Jesus,' and by 'nunc et in hora mortis nostrae.' But none of it was quite real. It was not satisfactory, somehow. She avoided her rosary, because, moving her with curious passion as it did, it *meant* only these not very significant things.... It was her instinct to put all these things away. It was her instinct to avoid thinking to avoid it, to save herself. (100).

This instinct to avoid thinking is at one with Anna's yearning for fully self-present meaning, a yearning that explains her initial attraction to Will Brangwen. Will's voice "thrills" Anna because it has the power to create the illusion of "Presence":

> [H]e spoke ... of nave and chancel and transept, of rood-screen and font, of hatchet-carving and moulding and tracery, speaking always with close passion of particular things.... It was a very real experience. She was carried away. And the land seemed to be covered with a vast, mystic church, reserved in gloom, thrilled with an unknown Presence. (108)

> His sentences were clumsy.... But he had the wonderful voice, that could ring its vibration through the girl's soul, transport her into his feeling.... She loved the running flame that coursed through her as she listened to him. (109)

No longer does Anna feel deferred and disappointed by words; no sterile substitute for sex, as Paul Morel's speech sometimes is, Will's talk is a form of sensuality providing a prelude to the fuller sexual experience of marriage. But ironically, by the time that their first-born is talking, words between Anna and Will are "only accidents in the mutual silence" (212) of their relationship. Will's mystic words are demystified through familiarity, and Anna seems entirely to turn her back upon the world of utterance—to become indifferent to the world of difference. She devotes herself to the production of children rather than to that of empty signifiers: "If her soul had found no utterance, her womb had" (203).

Anna's "practical indifference" to anything "extra-human" constitutes a ruthless rationalism and literalism that alienate her from the rest of her family. In them the longing for the eternal and the absolute—for some transcendental signified—remains profound as it was in Anna in her adolescence. Ursula's career partly recapitulates her mother's in that her encounters with Christian symbolism and with Scriptures leave her with a sense of the inadequacy of the Word—and of words. The sensuality of Ursula's struggles to close the gap between Sunday's "visions that had spoken far-off words that ran along the blood" and the materiality of the "weekday" world (282) intimates her longing for immediately self-present spiritual meaning: "[Christ] must gather her body to his breast, that was strong with a broad bone, and which sounded with the beating of the heart, and which was warm with the life of which she partook, the life of the running blood. . . . [S]he craved for the breast of the Son of Man, to lie there" (284). This "confused heat of religious yearning" (285) represents an attempt literally—physically—to embrace spiritual meaning incarnate.

Ursula's response to her failure to possess Christ thus in "everyday" terms is to admit the incommensurability of the relative and the absolute: "it was a betrayal, a transference of meaning, from the vision world, to the matter-of-fact world. So she was ashamed of her religious ecstasy . . . " (284). Similarly her failures to read the Scriptures literally force Ursula to revert to nonliteral interpretation, rationalizing: "What was this relation between a needle's eye, a rich man and heaven? . . . Who knows? It means the Absolute World, and can never be more than half interpreted in terms of the relative world" (275). Always a shadowy space—the gap or lag to which *différance* refers—opens between signifier and signified!

An analogous pattern informs the narrator's comment upon Ursula's disillusion with college: "Always the crest of the hill gleaming ahead under heaven: and then from the top of the hill only another sordid valley full of amorphous, squalid activity" (436). It is significant that at the point where the text makes this admission it also initiates a remarkable sequence of passages that implicitly affirm the symbolic conception of the sign. The first of these is the famous passage in which, disturbed by her professor's remark that there is no reason to "attribute some special mystery to life" (440), Ursula focuses on a microorganism under her microscope:

> For what purpose were the incalculable physical and chemical activities nodalised in this shadowy, moving speck under her microscope? What was the will which nodalised them and created the one thing she saw? What was its intention? To be itself? Was its purpose just mechanical and limited to itself?
>
> It intended to be itself. But what self? Suddenly in her mind the world gleamed strangely, with an intense light, like the nucleus of the creature under the microscope. Suddenly she had passed away into an intensely-gleaming light of knowledge. She could not understand what it all was. She only knew that it was not limited mechanical energy, nor mere purpose of self-preservation and self-assertion. It was a consummation, a being infinite. Self was a oneness with the infinite. To be oneself was a supreme, gleaming triumph of infinity.
>
> Ursula sat abstracted over her microscope. . . . Her soul was busy . . . in the new world . . . her soul was engaged. (441)

The terms employed here resemble those Lawrence uses to discuss the efficacy of astrological symbols in his review of *The Dragon of the Apocalypse*: the entry into the "zodiacal heavens," he writes, "is the entry into another world . . . measured by another dimension. And we find some prisoned self in us coming forth to live in this world" (P 293). The microorganism affects Ursula in much the same way that symbols, according to Lawrence, affect the perceiver: by arousing "the deep emotional self, the dynamic self, beyond comprehension" (P 296). The difficult statement that "Self [is] a oneness with the infinite" may be read as an affirmation of the infinity of the self in which the self stands in relation to the infinite as a symbol stands to the symbolized, as an entity partaking of that reality it represents. To assert the oneness of the self with the infinite is thus to affirm the symbolic conception of the sign, the possibility of the unity of signifier and signified.

This affirmation is reinforced through the realization or literalization of metaphors that occur earlier in the text when Ursula changes her course of study in college from French to biology. That this shift indicates a rejection of the spoken world—a substitution of nonhuman, wordless life for nonliving, human words—is clear not only from the laboratory scene but this passage of narrative commentary which precedes it:

> This world in which she lived was like a circle lighted by a lamp. This lighted area, lit up by man's completest consciousness, she thought was all the world.... Yet all the time, within the darkness she had been aware of points of light, like the eyes of wild beasts, gleaming, penetrating, vanishing....
>
> [Now] she could see the glimmer of dark movement just out of range, she saw the eyes of the wild beast gleaming from the darkness, watching the vanity of the campfire and the sleepers....
>
> [T]he darkness wheeled round about, with grey shadow-shapes of wild beasts, and also with dark shadow-shapes of the angels, whom the light fenced out, as it fenced out the more familiar beasts of darkness. And some [of the people gathered about the campfire], having for a moment seen the darkness, saw it bristling with the tufts of the hyena and the wolf; and some having given up their vanity of the light, having died in their own conceit, saw the gleam in the eyes of the wolf and the hyena, that it was the flash of the sword of angels, flashing at the door to come in, that the angels in the darkness were lordly and terrible and not to be denied, like the flash of fangs. (437–38)

Some of the metaphors in this passage are realized or given actuality in the experience of the characters when, after her revelation at the microscope, Ursula renews her relationship with Anton Skrebensky. Newly returned from Africa, Skrebensky is allied with darkness and becomes her means of exploring the "darkness" within herself, the creative unconscious that is symbolized through the metaphor of darkness in the passage quoted above. Skrebensky's voice exercises over Ursula the same kind of seductive power as "the eyes of the wild beast gleaming from the darkness" in the narrator's parable or allegory: "He was to her a voice out of the darkness. He talked to her all the while, in low tones, conveying something strange and sensual to her.... Gradually he transferred to her the hot, fecund darkness that possessed his own blood" (446). Drawn to "the fecundity of the universal night he inhabit[s]" (450), Ursula seems to identify Skrebensky with the angels of darkness; and the sexual drama enacted by the couple is one in which they are transformed into something like the beasts that lurk at the periphery of the "little lighted camp of vain, foolish sleepers." Their pacing mimes the pacing of those beasts in the jungle, both attracted by the light of the camp and and frightened by it: during their affair, they are constantly on the move, both seeking out and seeking escape from "'[t]he stupid lights'" of "'[t]he stupid, artificial, exaggerated town'" (448).

Near the end of their relationship Ursula enacts a savage "destruction" of her lover, entering a conflict with him which realizes or actualizes something like "the flash of the sword of angels ... like the flash of fangs." Visiting Lincolnshire (significantly, the site of Anna's destruction of Will's reverence for religious symbols in "The Cathedral"), Ursula is seized by "a yearning for something unknown" and becomes beastlike in her pursuit of it. The incandescence of the moon provokes "low, calling tones" (478) from her, as if from the wolf or hyena in her revery; and the description of her lovemaking with Skrebensky presents a struggle between two animalistic, primal creatures in which "her grip," her "fierce, beaked, harpy's kiss" "seemed to be pressing ... till she had the heart of him": "He came direct to her, without preliminaries. She held him pinned down at the chest, awful. The fight, the struggle for consummation was terrible" (479). The struggle concludes in a kind of death for both of them: Skrebensky feels "as if the knife were being pushed into his already dead body" (479), and Ursula wakes the next morning to "a new access of superficial life. But all within her was cold, dead, inert" (480).

Dramatized here is an agonizing failure to join signifier and signified. Ursula's effort symbolically to appropriate the darkness represented by Skrebensky through sexual union with him is doomed to failure because he is a mere cipher, an empty counter: "'You seem like nothing to me'" (309), Ursula says to him when she is sixteen; the rest of their relation is an attempt to deny that knowledge by her imbuing Skrebensky with spurious significance. He becomes for Ursula a signifier of her own potential, much as "the woman" becomes a signifier of the moral and spiritual potential of Ursula's male forebears. Their terrible consummation in Lincolnshire, which ends their relation, restores to Ursula the recognition of Skrebensky's nothingness and thus constitutes a recognition of the emptiness of the signifier.[9]

At the same time, the text resists that recognition through the literalization of metaphors that occurred earlier. The movement from abstract to concrete, from the purely metaphoric (that is, purely verbal or linguistic) beasts of the narrative commentary to the actual, animalistic conflict between the lovers (that is, symbolic action) may be read as a logocentric impulse, a reaching toward some actuality to which words refer. As an attempt to give substance to verbal formulations, literalization represents yet another textual effort to unite signifier with signified, another affirmation of the symbolic conception of the sign.

The symbolism in the episode describing Ursula's experience with the horses extends this effort, both by further literalizing aspects of earlier metaphors and by creating as vivid an impression of "presence" as any passage in the novel:

> She knew the heaviness on her heart. It was the weight of the horses. But she would circumvent them.... What was it that was drawing near her, what weight oppressing her heart?...[H]er way was cut off.... They would burst before her. They would burst before her.... In a sort of lightning of knowledge their movement travelled through her, the quiver and strain and thrust of their powerful flanks, as they burst before her and drew on, beyond.... She was aware of their breasts gripped, clenched narrow in a hold that never relaxed, she was aware of their red nostrils flaming with long endurance, and of their haunches, so rounded, so massive, pressing, pressing, pressing, to burst the grip upon their breasts, pressing forever till they went mad, running against the walls of time, and never bursting free.... She went on, drawing near. She was aware of the great flash of hoofs, a bluish, iridescent flash surrounding a hollow of darkness. Large, large seemed the bluish, incandescent flash of the hoof-iron, large as a halo of lightning round the knotted darkness of the flanks.... They were awaiting her again.... She must draw near. But they broke away.... They were behind her. The way was open before her, to the gate in the high hedge in the near distance, so she could pass into the smaller, cultivated field, and so out to the high-road and the ordered world of man.... Yet her heart was couched with fear.... Suddenly she hesitated as if seized by lightning.... The thunder of horses galloping down the path behind her shook her.... Cruelly, they swerved and crashed by on her left hand. She saw the fierce flanks crinkled and as yet inadequate, the great hoofs flashing bright as yet only brandished about her .... They had gone by, brandishing themselves thunderously about her, enclosing her. They slackened their burst transport.... That concentrated knitted flank of the horse-group had conquered. (487–88)

The rhythmic repetitions, even more apparent in the full passage, generate a powerful sense of the immediate presence of the horses. That the horses, whether real or hallucinatory, externalize Ursula's own passional energies confined, locked up, ever creating conflict and threatening destruction (a very real possibility should she marry Skrebensky for the sake of the child she now believes she is carrying) is plain from the way in which the terminology of this passage echoes that in the description of Ursula's terrible fight for consummation with Skrebensky ("clenched," "grip," "pressing," "flashing," "incandescent").

The imagery describing the horses also extends the literalization of metaphors that occurred earlier in the text: their "great hoofs flashing bright [that] as yet only brandished about her" do not merely evoke, but make concrete "the flash of the sword of angels ... like the flash of fangs." Though here we have neither angels nor fangs, the ambivalence represented by the simile pervades this episode, in Ursula's ambivalence toward the horses: there is a kind of attraction in their fearsomeness, and if she is afraid of the horses, she is also frightened by the prospect of passing "into the smaller cultivated field ... and the ordered world of man." Her hesitation on the point of escape and her thought that she "dare not draw near" both intimate that she wants to encounter, not escape, the animals; and once she has passed out of "danger," she feels as if "she must walk for the rest of her life, wearily, wearily.... [T]he monotony produced a deep, cold sense of nausea in her" (490), a feeling that arises not from her encounter with the horses but from the prospect of return to the "ordered world of man."

By dramatizing the ambivalence signified earlier by "the angels in the darkness lordly and terrible and not to be denied" (438), the text once more attempts to give substance—to give concrete form in the world presented by the novel—to linguistic formulations that occurred earlier. The ultimate example of such literalization is, of course, the rainbow that Ursula sees at the end of the novel. This rainbow is a concrete manifestation of the promise intimated earlier in the text through metaphoric appearances of the rainbow or rainbowlike figures. The sequential transformation of the arch and rainbow metaphors ultimately into the symbolic rainbow at the end of the novel in itself figures a process of growth that we might describe in terms of an organic metaphor: a development from the seed of the simile of a broken arch used to describe Tom Brangwen early in his marriage to Lydia (60) to the implied arch of their meeting "to the span of the heavens" (92) to the metaphoric rainbow under which Anna settles in the "builded house" (193) of her domesticity to the "fruition" of these figures in Ursula's rainbow. Such a pattern not only reinforces the metaphors of germination and growth in the last two paragraphs of the novel, but through proposing an "evolution" from simile to metaphor to symbol, through presenting symbol as the fulfillment or consummation of a certain linguistic pattern, valorizes the symbolic conception of the sign.

Two Narratives of the Self in *The Rainbow*

To say, as many readers have, that Ursula's vision of the rainbow is not "earned" is to say that this final affirmation fails to unite signifier and signified. If one is to be compelled by Ursula's vision of "the earth's new architecture, the old brittle corruption of houses and factories swept away, the world built up in a living fabric of Truth, fitting to the over-arching heaven" (495), one must be convinced of a "new germination" in Ursula which would ground the possibility of universal spiritual regeneration signified by the rainbow. But the authority of the organic metaphor is undermined by the way in which the text questions the conception of the self implied by that metaphor.

Ursula's transformation is signified by a dream she has in her delirium after her encounter with the stampeding horses:

And again, to her feverish brain, came the vivid reality of acorns in February lying on the floor of a wood with their shells burst and discarded and the kernel issued naked to put itself forth. She was the naked, clear kernel thrusting forth the clear, powerful shoot...and striving to take new root, to create a new knowledge of Eternity in the flux of Time. (492)

The opposition here between kernel (or core or center) and shell (or husk or rind or circumference) implies a core of unchanging and genuine identity in Ursula the existence of which was affirmed earlier, immediately after her encounter with the stampeding horses: "As she sat there, spent, time and the flux of change passed away from her, she lay as if unconscious upon the bed of the stream, like a stone, unconscious, unchanging, unchangeable, whilst everything rolled by in transience" (489). While each of these metaphors in its own way seeks to establish that Ursula possesses a "soul" or "absolute self," Lawrence's use of them nonetheless provokes a perplexing question: does Ursula possess this personal center or core of identity *because* of her experiences or *despite* them?

The Rainbow contains two narratives of the self which correspond to the two possibilities indicated by the question. One narrative posits a self that is a primal, intuitively known unity—a presence—which suffers deformation, disfiguration, and disintegration as a result of its relation to the other and yet nevertheless survives as that bedrock self that Ursula discovers, "like a stone, unconscious, unchanging, unchangeable." It is the confirmation of the hardihood of this self, not only by Ursula's experiences but by the vicissitudes of experience suffered by all the Brangwens, that is signified by the stone metaphor. This confirmation apparently opens the possibility of further growth, a possibility indicated by the seed metaphor. To speak of the growth from this seed, that is, to employ the organic metaphor, is but to use a different figure for that journey into the beyond which is the dominant metaphor in the presentation of all three generations of Brangwen experience. Each of the three metaphors—stone, seed, and journey—foregrounds a different aspect of the possibility of a permanent, continuous self.[10]

The second narrative of the self constitutes a threat to the first, and takes the form of an interrogation of the first. In the second narrative the possibility of a permanent, continuous self—or an organic self—is a delusion: rather the self is constituted in and through its differential relations to others, and is but an effect or a semblance derived from those relations. In light of this narrative of the self, the conception I outlined above—the organic conception—suffers deformation, disfiguration, and disintegration in Lawrence's text.

The organic conception can be plainly seen in the second half of the narrative, which presents Ursula's growth and development—and which, interestingly, was written before Lawrence added the narratives of Anna and

Will and Tom and Lydia.[11] (In other words, the generations were "conceived" in reverse order of that in which they appear in the novel, a fact which in itself undermines the idea of the kind of originary self intimated by the seed metaphor.) Although the terminology of the self in this part of the novel is extremely various, the proliferating terms do fall into a basic pattern of opposition between, on the one hand, what we might call the conscious, temporal self, and on the other hand, the unconscious, permanent self (the soul).

The former self is denoted by such terms as "everyday self" (452), "civic self" (449), "temporary social self" (453), and "relative self" (187). The latter is denoted by such terms as "dark, vital self" (449), "primal man" (462), "another, stronger self that knew the darkness," her "soul," "her permanent self" (452), "wild, chaotic soul" (407), "lower, deeper self" (69). The conscious, temporal self seems to be constituted of proliferating masks or roles, and stands in opposition to some permanent or absolute self to which Lawrence alternately gives the names "soul" and "unconscious." The most unusual feature of Lawrence's rendering here of what is a fundamentally traditional model of the self is his identification of the individual's instincts with the soul, an identification accomplished in *The Rainbow* through the privileging of sexual relationships and marriage as means to fulfillment and then through Ursula's ecstatic observation of the microorganism under her microscope, where she learns to define the transcendent in terms of the biological.

One peculiarity of that scene which we have not yet noted is that almost as soon as she discovers that "Self [is] a oneness with the infinite," Ursula literally leaps from her labstool to seek the Other:

> A great craving to depart came upon her. . . . She was in dread of the material world, and in dread of her own transfiguration. She wanted to run to meet Skrebensky—the new life, the new reality. . . . [I]t would be a new beginning. . . . [S]he would not admit to herself the chill like a sunshine of frost that came over her [when she spotted Skrebensky in the corridor]. This was he, the key, the nucleus to the new world. (442)

Ursula's behavior here hints at her dependence upon the other (Skrebensky) for a sense of self or identity; and it highlights the ambiguity of "Self [is] a oneness with the infinite": not only can the sentence be read as an affirmation of the autonomy and the infinite potential of the self; it can be read as an assertion of the self's absolute dependence on all that is not self for its constitution. In its ambiguity, then, the sentence embraces both models of the self informing the novel. The second reading recalls a difficulty introduced much earlier in the text, where Skrebensky and the adolescent Ursula make "a delicious, exciting game" (300) of playing at kisses:

[S]omething was roused in both of them that they could not now allay. It intensified and heightened their senses, they were more vivid, and powerful in their being. But under it all was a poignant sense of transience. It was a magnificent self-assertion on the part of both of them, he asserted himself before her, he felt himself infinitely male and infinitely irresistible, she asserted herself before him, she knew herself infinitely desirable, and hence infinitely strong. And after all, what could either of them get from such a passion but a sense of his or her own maximum self, in contradistinction to all the rest of life? Wherein was something finite and sad, for the human soul at its maximum wants a sense of the infinite. (301)

In its insistence that the characters need each other in order to know themselves "in contradistinction to all the rest of life," the passage presupposes the differential model of the self. At the same time, the passage comments upon the painful human limitations exposed by that model: "a sense of the infinite" is incompatible with any notion of the self that defines identity not as a matter of essence but as a matter of differentiation from the other.

The sense of "something finite and sad" persistently qualifies the affirmations of *The Rainbow* and accompanies its implicit interrogation of the possibility of an essential self anterior to and independent of one's relations to the world. One means by which the text conducts this interrogation is through metaphors that provoke uncertainty as to the "location" of the self. Such uncertainty pervades the opening chapter of *The Rainbow,* where we learn that Tom Brangwen has inherited his forebears' attitudes toward women, attitudes in which "the woman"—the other—stands as a symbol of all that is "beyond" the emotional or spiritual capacities of the individual Brangwen male:

In the close intimacy of the farm kitchen, the woman occupied the supreme position. The men deferred to her in the house, on all household points, on all points of morality and behaviour. The woman was the symbol for that further life which comprised religion and love and morality. The men placed in her hands their own conscience. . . . They depended on her for their stability. . . . She was the anchor and the security, she was the restraining hand of God, at times highly to be execrated. (13)

Here it seems that in their relationship to "the woman," the Brangwen men symbolically appropriate what they lack: "religion and love and morality." But at the same time, it might be said that the Brangwen woman expropriates the "conscience" of the men (by taking it "in her hands"). Where *are* the religious or moral sensibilities of the Brangwen men? Does each possess a conscience that he relinquishes to the woman, or does he come into possession of a conscience through his relation with the woman? Such questions proliferate when we read of Tom: "The disillusion of his first carnal contact with woman, strengthened by his innate desire to find in a woman the embodiment of all his inarticulate, powerful religious impulses, put a bit in his mouth. He had something to lose which he was afraid of losing, which he was not sure even of possessing" (14). Here it seems that Tom's reverential attitude toward "woman" derives from a need to see articulated that which is inarticulate within him ("all his inarticulate, powerful religious impulses"), yet a note of doubt about his "possession" of those impulses enters the second sentence.

An important uncertainty thus arises in this chapter. At times, the text implies that the other symbolizes to the Brangwens that which is unknown or unrealized within the self. As a consequence, to embrace "the beyond" or the other can be to "find" oneself, to uncover a self that exists prior to the discovery, that is, a self existing prior to consciousness. At other points, however, the implication is that the self evolves through symbolic appropriation of what it lacks, amplifying itself at the same time it comes to know itself as its own insufficiency in contradistinction to the other; in this case, all self would be consciousness of absence.

The play between these possibilities is also evident in the account of Tom's first encounters with Lydia Lensky, where Lydia's intrusion upon Tom's accustomed landscape transports him to "a far world, the fragile reality," "the world that was beyond reality" (24).[12] The equivocal use of "reality" here indicates, on the one hand, that the beyond is not quite real—its "reality" is "fragile"—precisely because it is unknown to Tom and, on the other hand, that Tom's own world is not quite real to him, that reality is the property of the beyond. Such equivocation as to the "location" of reality generates a sense of instability in the passage which undermines its implicit claim that Tom has "found" himself: "A swift change had taken place on the earth for him, as if a new creation were fulfilled, in which he had real existence. Things had all been stark, unreal, barren, mere nullities before. Now they were actualities he could handle" (26). Tom's sense of his own reality, his "self-realization," appears to depend upon an encounter with "actualities" outside himself. But has some change occurred within him that enables him to perceive those actualities, or is the change in the outward world, which is now inhabited by that foreign element, Lydia? That Tom "dared not know" the woman herself (27), the other whose presence has brought about "the swift change," is a reticence suggesting that Tom's new-found "real existence" depends so entirely on the other, on the unknown, that to make her known constitutes a threat to his identity or selfhood.

Yet, through a sequence of contradictions and paradoxes, the passage obscures at the same time that it discloses the importance of absence. After presenting the "swift change that had taken place on the earth for [Tom]," the text retreats to claim that Tom still awaits transformation: "The world was submitting to its transformation. He made no move: it would come, what would come" (26). In addition, Lydia is presented as both immediately present and distant: "all the time he was aware of her presence not far off, he lived in her" (27). Tom is both "in" her and "outside" her. Finally, the attribution of power in this section is equivocal. The narrative both insists upon the transforming power of Tom's vision (i.e., that the change comes from within him) and upon the approach of the transformation from the beyond.

Such dubieties create an effect that resembles Tom's almost ecstatic response to the foreign gentleman—another manifestation of the beyond or other—whom he meets at Matlock: "his whole being [was] in a whirl. . . . What was this that he had touched? What was he in this new influence? What did everything mean? Where was life, in that which he knew or all outside him?" (19). Where is the self—"inside" or "outside"? By posing this question, not only in this passage but through the rhetoric of the account of Lydia's entry into Tom's world, the novel moves toward collapsing the important dichotomy of inner and outer upon which the organic conception of the self depends.

Ironically, nowhere in the novel are the uncertainty and disorientation as to inner and outer more pronounced than at that point where Lawrence most emphatically insists that Tom and Lydia have established themselves in marriage:[13]

> She was there, if he could reach her. The reality of her who was just beyond him absorbed him. Blind and destroyed, he pressed forward, nearer, nearer, to receive the consummation of himself, he received within the darkness which should swallow him and yield him up to himself. If he could really come within the blazing kernel of darkness, if really he could be destroyed, burnt away until he lit with her in one consummation, that were supreme, supreme.
>
> Their coming together now, after two years of married life, was much more wonderful to them than it had been before. It was the entry into another circle of existence, it was the baptism to another life, it was the complete confirmation. Their feet trod strange ground of knowledge, their footsteps were lit up with discovery. Wherever they walked, it was well, the world re-echoed round them in discovery. . . . Everything was lost, and everything was found. The new world was discovered, it remained only to be explored. (90–91)

The verbal yoking of opposites—darkness and light, inner and outer—seeks to justify the terminology of religious mystery in this passage, and to a certain extent the oxymorons and paradoxes command our assent to the spiritual claim being made here: that the characters have discovered wholeness of being in and through their marriage. Yet as the paradoxes replace each other in rapid succession, the effect is disorienting. Lydia is "there," "just beyond him," yet he is "in" her (for she "absorb[s] him"). He wants to come "*within* the blazing kernel of darkness" (my emphasis), yet they move *out* "into another circle of existence" where their "footsteps were lit up with discovery." Then we read:

> They had passed through the doorway into the further space, where movement was so big, that it contained bonds and constraints and labours, and still was complete liberty. She was the doorway to him, he to her. At last they had thrown open the doors, each to the other, and had stood in the doorways facing each other, whilst the light flooded out from behind on to each of their faces, it was the transfiguration, glorification, the admission. (91)

The doorway metaphors here are perplexing. On the one hand, each of the characters seems to be liberated and enlarged by passing "through the doorway into the further space" of the other. On the other hand, the characters are each in a sense reduced to a subordinate or mediating position in relation to the other ("She was the doorway to him, he to her"), and they seem to be suspended or confined in the doorways in which they stand "facing each other." Not even the source of light is firmly situated here: it is both inside and outside the characters. The light "flood[s] out from *behind* on to each of their faces" and yet "the light [is that] of the transfiguration [which] burned on *in* their hearts" (91, emphasis added).

The fire is that of God declaring himself to the couple: "When at last they had joined hands, the house was finished, and the Lord took up his abode" (91–92). The architectural metaphors, which would seem to signify stability, actually introduce an undecidable question about that stability. The text presents what we might call a "founding moment" in the relation of Tom and Lydia, but is it the case here that the self is founded upon the ground of the marriage or that the marriage is founded upon the ground of the self? The ambiguity qualifies the notion of stability, as do further prepositional ambiguities in the narrative: "she was *with* him, *near* him ... she was the gateway and the way *out* ... she was *beyond,* and ... he was travelling *in her through the beyond.* Whither?—What does it matter? He responded always. When she called, he answered, when he asked, her response came at once, or at length" (92, emphasis added). *Or at length*: the qualification has the effect of rendering unstable the whole structure of parallelisms being erected here, an effect undermining our confidence in the structure announced in the next paragraph, where we learn that Anna "saw them established to her safety.... Her father and mother now met to the span of the heavens, and she ... was free to play in the space beneath, between" (92).

Such triumphant assertions are further undermined by the abstractness of the language throughout the passage. "Consummation," "baptism," "confirmation," "knowledge," "discovery," "transfiguration," "glorification," "admission," "perpetual wonder," "complete liberty"—such terminology makes Tom and Lydia invisible, rendering their presence insignificant even as it attempts to "enlarge" them. The whirl of abstractions the passage places between reader and characters provides a rhetorical or textual analogue not only to the whirl in Tom's mind after he meets the stranger at Matlock but also to the image of the "roaring vast space" in Tom's revery on Anna's wedding day:

He felt himself tiny, a little upright figure on a plain circle[d] round with the immense roaring sky: he and his wife, two little upright figures walking across this plain, whilst the heavens shimmered and roared about them. When did it come to an end? In which direction was it finished? There was no end, no finish, only this roaring vast space. Did one never get old, never die? That was the clue. He exulted strangely, with torture. He would go on with his wife, he and she like two children camping in the plains. What was sure but the endless sky? But that was so sure, so boundless. (131)

The passage not only discloses Tom's sense of personal insignificance but indicates that the "surety" he locates is the certainty of death, of material submersion and dispersion in "the infinite." No mere reflections of Tom's uncertainty and insecurity, the repetitions of "sure" hark back to the "surety" associated with the Brangwens on the first page of the novel, where we read that they "had that air of readiness for what would come to them, a kind of surety, an expectancy, the look of an inheritor." Ambiguously referring both to the ancestral self-assurance of the Brangwens (a kind of assurance that oddly contradicts their dramatized behavior) and to the promise offered by the beyond, that "surety" is reduced through Tom's experience to the promise of death. This promise is fulfilled in "The Marsh and the Flood," where the impersonal force of nature, so lyrically presented in the opening pages of the novel as "the wave which cannot halt" (2), reaches out to claim Tom, whose immortality lies not in achieved individuality, but in his virtual identification with the infinite. Such a death is surely not what Ursula has in mind in thinking that "Self [is] a oneness with the infinite," but rather almost parodies as it literalizes the meaning of her metaphor.

This literalization of Tom's "insignificance," of his nothingness in the face of the overwhelming forces of the unknown, retrospectively urges upon us an ironic reading of some of the claims made in the transfiguration passage: "she was beyond, and . . . he was travelling in her through the beyond. Whither?—What does it matter?" (92). *He was travelling in her through the beyond*: the words indicate that Tom's union with Lydia takes the form of a kind of submersion in the infinite as it is symbolized to him by his wife. Lydia's relation to the infinite deserves close scrutiny:

> She had some beliefs *somewhere,* never defined. . . . The outward form [of religion] was a matter of indifference to her. Yet she had some fundamental religion. It was as if she worshipped God as a mystery, never seeking to define what He was.
> And *inside* her, the subtle sense of the Great Absolute *wherein* she had her being was very strong. The English dogma never reached her: the language was too foreign. *Through it all* she felt the great Separator who held life *in* His hands, gleaming, imminent, terrible, the Great Mystery, *immediate beyond all telling.*
> She shone and gleamed *to* the Mystery, Whom she knew *through* all her senses, she glanced with strange, mystic superstitions that never found expression in the English language, never mounted to thought in English. But so she lived, *within* a potent, sensuous belief that included her family and contained her destiny.

> *To this she had reduced her husband.* He existed with her entirely indifferent to the
> general values of the world. Her very ways, the very mark of her eyebrows were symbols and
> indication to him. (99, emphasis added)

The bewildering play of prepositions here not only creates the effect of the elusiveness of Lydia's beliefs but also creates ambiguity as to the location of *her being,* an ambiguity that extends the web of perplexities in the presentation of her relation with Tom. Like so much of *The Rainbow,* the passage seems to disclose at the same time that it rejects the possibility that the Absolute is not "beyond," but enmeshed in a net of differences which constitute language and reality.

Lydia's sense of a direct or immediate apprehension of the Absolute jars uncomfortably against the suggestion that it is merely because of her refusal to define and her fuzzy knowledge of her husband's native language that she is able to keep alive the Mystery, the illusion of Presence. The strangely ambiguous, "Through it all she felt the great Separator..." ("it" can refer to her life with Tom or the English language), and the curiously paradoxical phrase, "the great Mystery, immediate beyond all telling," adumbrate at the same time that they attempt to conceal the possibility that the great Presence can be defined only in terms of absence. That we are not to read this possibility merely as a religious paradox enhancing the mystery of the Absolute is clear when we notice that the relation between Tom and Lydia posited by this passage duplicates the relation between Tom's male ancestors and "the woman": "Her very ways, the very mark of her eyebrows were symbols and indication to him." The novel thus poses with regard to Lydia the same question that it poses with regard to the Ur-Brangwen "woman": Is she authentic symbol or empty sign?

The uncertainty may not constitute her mystery for Tom, but the question is one whose larger implications the novel addresses in the section presenting the marriage of Anna and Will Brangwen. That section explores the question through Anna's jeering at Will's attachment to conventional religious symbols. To Will, for example, the Pietà "'means the Sacraments, the Bread.... [I]t's Christ.... You've got to take it [the image] for what it means'" (157); to Anna "'It means your human body put up to be slit and killed and then worshipped'" (158). To Will, the image of the lamb in the church window is "'the symbol of Christ, of his Innocence and sacrifice'"; to Anna, "'it's a *lamb,*'" and she "'like[s] lambs too much to treat them as if they had to mean something'" (158). The conflict dramatized by these arguments leads Will to "forfeit from his soul all his symbols" (159), its climax occurring in Lincoln Cathedral. There Anna counteracts Will's ecstatic response to the interior of the building by pointing at the jeering faces on some carvings: "They knew quite well, these little imps that retorted on man's illusion, that the cathedral was not absolute. They winked and leered, giving suggestion of the many things that had been left out of the great concept of the church" (201). Such passages may "retort on" Tom's willingness to embrace the absolute symbolically through Lydia: perhaps he should like Lydia too much to treat her as if she had to mean something, even the great Mystery.

Like the experiences of Tom and Lydia, those of Anna and Will support Tedlock's view that the "psychic stages" through which the characters pass "constitute a search for the absolute in a world of disastrous relativity and unreligiousness" (87). At the same time, however, this search is questioned by their experiences. Anna and Will, like Tom and Lydia, each enact a kind of submersion in the infinite that literalizes or gives materiality to Ursula's metaphor, "Self [is] a oneness with the infinite"; and as is the case with the first generation, that literalization has two different but related effects: it exposes the limitations of the characters at the same time that it tests the validity of Ursula's notion. A version of that notion occurs in the passage describing the honeymoon of Anna and Will. The passage presents a counterpart of the transfiguration (or founding moment) of Lydia and Tom, an experience where the characters enter what Lawrence calls the fourth dimension ("Morality and the Novel," P 527) then reenter the three-dimensional world transformed by the transcendent reality:

> Inside the room was a great steadiness, a core of living eternity. Only far outside, at the rim, went on the noise and the destruction. Here at the centre the great wheel was motionless, centred upon itself. Here was poised, unflawed stillness that was beyond time, because it remained the same, inexhaustible, unchanging, unexhausted.
> As they lay close together, complete and beyond the touch of time or change, it was as if they were at the very centre of all the slow wheeling of space and the rapid agitation of life, deep, deep inside them all, at the centre where there is utter radiance, and eternal being, and the silence absorbed in praise.... They found themselves there, and they lay still, in each other's arms; for their moment they were at the heart of eternity, whilst time roared far off, forever far off, towards the rim.
> Then gradually they were passed away from the supreme centre, down the circles of praise and joy and gladness, further and further out, towards the noise and friction. But their hearts had burned and were tempered by the inner reality, they were unalterably glad. (141)

The assumptions concerning the self in this passage are similar to those informing the passage in which Ursula is described in terms of "the naked, clear [acorn] kernel" (492). The terminology opposing center and circumference, inner and outer, eternality and temporality, reality and illusion is associated with the view that the self has a permanent or fixed center from which emanate all the activities of the individual. The claim that "they found themselves there," of course, assumes a preexisting self to be discovered at the still point or the center of "the slow wheeling of space." A secondary, punning suggestion of the term "found" is that Anna and Will ground or found themselves "there" at the center. Their marriage, however, provokes skepticism as to the validity of the notion of foundedness. The intensity of the conflicts that arise between the two young people reflects their individual senses of incompleteness, their deep fear and resentment of being dependent upon the other for a sense of foundedness and completion.

The true transfigurations or founding moments in this section of the novel are scenes in which the characters acquire a sense of their own completeness by *obliterating* rather than embracing the other. One such scene is that in which Anna celebrates the measure of independence from Will that maternity brings by removing her clothes to dance pregnant and alone in the firelight:

> He [Will] was in the house, so her pride was fiercer. She would dance his nullification, she would dance to her unseen Lord. She was exalted over him, before the Lord. . . . [S]he lifted her hands and danced again, to annul him. . . . [S]he swayed backwards and forwards . . . dancing his non-existence. . . . (180)

Such nullification is not sufficient to create in Anna a permanent sense of a stable, founded self; her ability to reproduce herself or multiply herself physically through childbearing thus takes on special importance for her,[14] an importance confirmed by architectural metaphors that occur later in the text:

> With satisfaction she relinquished the adventure to the unknown. She was bearing her children. . . . If she were not the wayfarer to the unknown, if she were arrived now, settled in her builded house, a rich woman, still her doors opened under the arch of the rainbow, her threshold reflected the passing of the sun and moon, the great travellers, her house was full of the echo of journeying.
>
> She was a door and threshold, she herself. Through her another soul was coming, to stand upon her as upon the threshold, looking out, shading its eyes for the direction to take. (193)

The stability and foundedness claimed here are measures of Anna's actual unfoundedness and insecurity. It is as if she must repeatedly confirm her own substance by externalizing it. Her compulsion to do so not only provides her a material means of submerging or immersing herself in the infinite but also constitutes a doubt about the substantiality of the self.

The repetitiveness of Anna's childbearing is matched by the almost compulsively reiterated claim that Will has found or founded (or established) himself, and the reiteration casts into doubt at the same time that it asserts the existence of an "absolute" self in Will. The term "absolute self" is, ironically, introduced in an episode that implicitly contradicts this idea. After Anna, during her first pregnancy, forces Will to sleep in a different room at times, Will finally comes into his own existence. He was born for a second time, born at last unto himself, out of the vast body of humanity. Now at last he had a separate identity, he existed alone, even if he were not quite alone. Before he had only existed in so far as he had relations with another being. Now he had an absolute self—as well as a relative self. (187)

The passage plainly presents the "absolute self" as the self that exists independently of all relations with the other, but it is, ironically, precisely through his relation with Anna that he acquires this "absolute self": he comes into being only through her rejection of him.

If Anna's motherhood represents a peculiar realization of the metaphor of losing oneself to find oneself, so does Will's relationship to her. Ultimately denied access to the Absolute through the Church, Will finally finds himself by losing himself in Absolute Beauty as made available to him by Anna's body. By giving himself "with infinite sensual violence . . . to the realisation of this supreme, immoral, Absolute Beauty, in the body of woman" (234), Will liberates in himself "another man," one who "wanted to be unanimous with the whole of purposive mankind": "He had at length, from his profound sensual activity, developed a real purposive self" (235). That is, the "heavy, fundamental gratification" provided by "their most unlicensed pleasures" grounds Will's being so that he begins "to find himself free to attend to the outside life as well" (235). Just as Anna's exultation in maternity excludes, indeed obliterates, Will even though he is her partner in parenthood, so does Will's "infinite, maddening intoxication of the sense" ultimately exclude Anna. Ironically, like Tom before them, Anna and Will each open a gap between self and other through using the other as a means of entering the infinite.

The Limits of the Organic and the Dangers of Consummation

Tom's drowning, viewed as a symbolic event dramatizing Tom's personal insignificance or the personal oblivion he enacts through "sinking" himself in his wife, exposes the limits of symbolism (and of the organic metaphysic with which it is associated), for every reader knows what Tom knows, that he both is and is not insignificant. As Anna's wedding approaches, Tom ponders his life in a revery that reveals the double view of Tom to which I am referring:

What was missing in his life, that, in his ravening soul, he was not satisfied? . . . What had he done? . . .

Was his life nothing? Had he nothing to show, no work? He did not count his work, anybody could have done it. What had he known, but the long, marital embrace with his wife! Curious, that this was what his life amounted to! At any rate it was something, it was eternal. He would say so to anybody, and be proud of it. He lay with his wife in his arms, and she was still his fulfilment, just the same as ever. And that was the be-all and the end-all. Yes, and he was proud of it. (124)

"At any rate, it was something, it was eternal"; "And that was the be-all and the end-all": such statements equivocate about the value of Tom's life, and the equivocation reflects a dual standard operating in the novel, a duplicity at which Eugene Goodheart glances when he writes: "In light of the transcendent nature of the consummations between the men and the women, the novel's sense of the inadequacy of the loves is somewhat puzzling" (120). One is tempted to ascribe this duplicity to the "dialogue of self and soul" that Edward Engelberg sees in the novel, "a dialectic between the character's objective experience and his subjective assimilation of it" (107). Tom's life is little enough or nothing according to the "objective" standards of the "everyday" world, but the self he acquires through "the long marital embrace" feels "eternal." From such a perspective, Lawrence's "most unusual insight into and respect for the heroic capacities of human feeling" (Alldritt 135), one might argue, dictates a hopeful or triumphant tone even where the text boldly underscores the limitations of the characters. Is not such ambivalence, one might ask, a natural part of human experience?

It is a great temptation, in writing about *The Rainbow,* to assimilate its ambivalences to some "natural" pattern. If we view the novel as structured by the two opposing impulses that inform the opening of the novel (the impulse toward union with the world of natural process and the impulse toward individuation through utterance in the world of human action and culture), it is difficult *not* to imply that this pattern of double impulse, or "double rhythm" (Ford 16 et passim), constitutes an "organic" pattern. And the novel justifiably inspires phrases like "rhythmic movement of recurrent promises and partial achievements" (Cavitch 53), language that derives its force from a correspondence to the powerful description, at the beginning of the novel, of the Brangwen men's relation to the soil. The recurrent promise of spring, the partial achievement of crops pulled from the furrow that "lies hard and unresponsive"—these structure the experience of the Brangwen *men* for generations. The alternations of viewpoint, theme, or whatever, when subsumed under the rubric of "natural" process or rhythm, then rather easily come to constitute the "organic unity" of the novel; that is, organic unity is certified by some critical assertion to the effect that the novel imitates the patterns of organic life in the natural world.

But to use the analogy with natural process to describe the form of the novel or to argue for its "wholeness" is to privilege the experience of the *male* Brangwen ancestors and superimpose upon the novel as a whole a pattern offered by the novel itself as limited, partial. The limitations of the organic are even evident in one of the most memorably "organic" passages in *The Rainbow*—the sheaf-stacking scene during the courtship of Anna and Will. This scene might be viewed as a linguistic effort to insist that the sexual consummations of the Brangwens are absolute by grounding those consummations in, or associating them with, "eternal" natural process. The virtual abolition of speech in this passage is a way of resisting difference, and the various sorts of rhythmic repetition implicitly attempt to ground the dancelike movements of Anna and Will in the cycles, the ebb and flow, of natural process. Like many of the other dramatically symbolic scenes of the novel, the famous sheaf-stacking scene might also be viewed as a great affirmation of the symbolic conception of the sign; the movements of the characters as they stack the sheaves so closely approximate, indeed participate in, the sexual reality they represent (the act of sexual intercourse) that one is tempted to agree with the critic who writes of the novel in general that "the rhythms of feeling are not merely like the rhythms of nature, but . . . they are essentially the same; or, more accurately, . . . the human pattern is a variant of the basic and inclusive natural pattern" (Berthoud 60).

We must remember, however, that the scene dramatizes an effort to close up a space: "Why was there always a space between them, why were they apart?" (118). The question should intimate to us that the scene is proleptic of Ursula's savage destruction of Skrebensky near the end of the novel. That later scene may be viewed as a failed effort to close the gap between signifier and signified—and the failure may actually be viewed as Ursula's salvation since it ends her empty relation with Skrebensky. In the earlier scene involving Anna and Will, however, the gap *is* finally closed, and when it is, "Something fixed in [Will] forever" (120). The moment of union, of possession, constitutes an ambiguous victory, for the deficiency in Will that we learn about later is precisely his being "fixed": "Something undeveloped in him limited him, there was a darkness in him which he could not unfold, which would never unfold in him" (207).

The denial of difference and absence is thus inextricably linked in *The Rainbow* to a sense of the dangers of consummation, of the Absolute, of fixity, a sense which troubles all the affirmations of the novel. It is to these dangers that Lawrence more fixedly directs his attention in *Women in Love*.

4

Going into the Abyss: Literalization in *Women in Love*

The differential metaphysic in *The Rainbow* proves irrepressible despite the ways in which the text appears to deny or resist its presence. Lawrence's next novel, *Women in Love,* more openly explores the implications of that metaphysic. Figuring difference and absence—spacing—as the abyss, Lawrence's novel is a complex web of permutations of that figure.

The Abyss as Fecund Void

What do we do when we reach the edge of an abyss? We may retrace our steps and attempt to return to our point of departure or origin; or we may retreat to remap the territory, replot the journey, take stock of our resources. Perhaps we then gather courage and strength to leap the abyss. Or we may be arrested on the brink of the void, where we balance ourselves, peer over the edge, and dream of transportation. Possibly we lose our balance—or wish to lose our balance. We may dream of flight. We may see our lives figured in the void. Perhaps we take risks that leave us dangling over the edge. We may descend a slope and emerge safely on the far side of a valley. We may descend a slope, lose our way, and die. In short, confronted by an abyss, we either stand still or keep going, and we can do so in innumerable ways. Each way is a story; the void is, paradoxically, full of narrative possibilities. Some of these possibilities weave the text of *Women in Love.*

More than one abyss opens in the first chapter as the Brangwen sisters talk about marriage, what Gudrun rather wearily and bitterly calls "'the inevitable next step'" in their lives. Spaces of silence, suppressed emotion, repeatedly break a conversation which finally closes after Gudrun is trapped by one of her own metaphors. When she remarks that she has returned home "'reculer pour mieux sauter,'" her sister asks, "'But where can one jump to?'":

> "Oh, it doesn't matter," said Gudrun, somewhat superbly. "If one jumps over the edge, one is bound to land somewhere."
> "But isn't it very risky?" asked Ursula.
> A slow mocking smile dawned on Gudrun's face.
> "Ah!" she said laughing. "What is it all but words!" And so again she closed the conversation. (4)

Gudrun characteristically uses words to the same end that she wears her remarkable, flamboyant clothes: to create an effect or to project an image of herself that hides her vulnerability. But her language here uncovers precisely the issue she has attempted to cover up: the frightening indeterminacy of her future. The rhetorical intention of her question—"What is it all but words!"—is undone when the figure of an abyss, implicit in her flippant answer to Ursula, is made explicit by the narrator: "The sisters found themselves confronted by a void, a terrifying chasm, as if they had looked over the edge" (4). Not only does the metaphor expose what the sisters, especially Gudrun, have attempted to suppress in and by their conversation—their fear; one might reasonably claim that the figure issues in, indeed generates, the landscape and action of the novel.

When Gudrun says she has returned to Beldover "'reculer pour mieux sauter,'" it is as if she intends to avoid "'the inevitable next step'"—marriage—and leap beyond the chasm that the avoiding creates. Her trajectory through the novel literalizes such a leap, an unsuccessful one which ends with her on her knees on the floor of an Alpine Valley, stunned by Gerald's attempt on her life; as he goes on to climb to his death, he gets his last glimpse of her, "dropped on her knees, like one executed" (464) where he left her in the chasm below. Viewed in connection with this pattern, the "strange transport" (9) that possesses Gudrun in the first chapter, as she views Gerald at the wedding, assumes special significance; the term "strange transport" is a pun that reveals Gudrun's dream of transportation across the abyss, a sinister dream progressively but incompletely realized by her relationship with Gerald.

Although Gerald climbs a slope to leave Gudrun behind at the end of the novel, he dies in a "hollow basin of snow, surrounded by sheer slopes and precipices" (466). Gerald's death in that hollowed-out space literalizes a metaphor that occurs earlier when, after his father's death, Gerald feels "like a man hung in chains over the edge of an abyss. Struggle as he might . . . he could not get footing. . . . There was no escape, there was nothing to grasp hold of" (330). At the end of "Snowed-Up," Gerald actually loses his footing and, as Birkin sees later, fails to find a nearby guide-rope that might have led to safety.

Gerald's journey into the abyss might indeed have proved his salvation. Visiting the site of Gerald's death, Birkin meditates upon the possibility that Gerald might have found that guide-rope and hauled himself to the crest of the mountain and safety: "He might have gone on, down the steep, steep fall of the southside, down into the dark valley with its pines, on to the great Imperial road leading south to Italy" (469). That the salvation Birkin imagines for his dead friend leads through a dark valley entails one of the many transvaluations of the metaphor of an abyss in the novel. Even in the first chapter, the implications of the metaphor are multiple.[1] On the one hand, the figure takes the form of a terrifying void that threatens to swallow the individual, not only in the scene where the Brangwen sisters discuss the future, but also in the description of Hermione Roddice, whose sense of personal wholeness and sufficiency is "built over a chasm," a "bottomless pit of insufficiency" (11). On the other hand, an allied metaphor hints at the fecundity of the void: Ursula's "active living was suspended, but underneath, in the darkness, something was coming to pass.... She seemed to try and put her hands out like an infant in the womb..." (3–4).

Throughout the novel, the meanings of the metaphor oscillate between, but are not strictly limited to, the two poles of creation and destruction intimated here, and the settings that issue from these metaphors show a corresponding oscillation in value. That is, landscape is multivalent or equivocal in *Women in Love*. So, for example, the English Channel is "a gulf of darkness," "the chasm between...worlds," an "ineffable rift" (379) in which Birkin locates peace even as he crosses it: "This was the first time that an utter and absolute peace had entered his heart, now, in this final transit out of life" (379). This peaceful way "out," however, is only a way "in" again, a way into the great cul-de-sac in the snow where Birkin gives up "absolute peace" to indulge in "an ecstasy of physical motion" (411). A similar irony is present when Birkin imagines a trip to Italy as a possible escape from the cul-de-sac. The symbolic promise of a journey southward is compromised by the implications of the dark valley through which Birkin must travel to Italy, so that he asks himself, "The south? Italy? What then? Was it a way out? It was only a way in again.... Was it any good going south, to Italy?" (469).

The permutations of the figure of an abyss create a self-questioning movement in the novel that is further illustrated by two successive passages that juxtapose Ursula and Gudrun's experiences of arrival in the Alpine valley. As Ursula stands in the valley she thinks:

Oh, God, could one bear it, this past which was gone down the abyss?... She wanted to have no past. She wanted to have come down the slopes of heaven to this place, with Birkin, not to have toiled out of the murk of her childhood and her upbringing, slowly, all soiled. She felt that memory was a dirty trick played upon her. What was this decree, that she should "remember"! Why not a bath of pure oblivion, a new birth, without any recollections or blemish of a past life. She was with Birkin, she had just come into life, here in the high snow, against the stars. What had she to do with parents and antecedents? She knew herself new and unbegotten, she had no father, no mother, no anterior connections, she was herself, pure and silvery, she belonged only to the oneness with Birkin, a oneness that struck deeper notes, sounding into the heart of the universe, the heart of reality, where she had never existed before. (399–400)

The "oneness with Birkin" that Ursula experiences in "this cradle of snow" (398) entails a number of paradoxes: she is born anew, yet "unbegotten"; she is one with Birkin, part of a unity—and yet herself, an individual "pure and silvery"; the valley in which she stands is not a place to which she has descended but to her regret a place to which she has toiled upward.

Despite these paradoxes, Ursula's "oneness with Birkin" stands in distinct contrast to the "oneness" that Gudrun yearns for as she explores the Alpine landscape:

> Then she wanted to climb the wall of white finality, climb over, into the peaks that sprang up like sharp petals in the heart of the frozen, mysterious navel of the world. She felt that there, over the strange blind, terrible wall of rocky snow, there in the navel of the mystic world, among the final cluster of peaks, there, in the infolded navel of it all, was her consummation. If she could but come there, alone, and pass into the infolded navel of eternal snow and of uprising, immortal peaks of snow and rock, she would be a oneness with all, she would be herself the eternal, infinite silence, the sleeping, timeless, frozen centre of the All. (400)

Gudrun's desire to "be a oneness with all" is a deadly alternative to the oneness that Ursula experiences with Birkin; it is a wish for death, for a union with the physical landscape that will allow her to escape the agonizing tensions of her relationship with Gerald.

Two uses of the term "heart" reinforce the contrast between Ursula's wish for a "bath of pure oblivion, a new birth" and Gudrun's desire for oblivion. Gudrun's "heart of the frozen, mysterious navel of the world" has little to do with Ursula's "heart of the universe, the heart of reality." It is, rather, a massive literalization of a figure that occurs in Ursula's revery, when she thinks of "this past which has gone down the abyss." As Ursula continues to think, she realizes that "Even Gudrun was a separate unit, separate, separate, having nothing to do with this self, this Ursula, in her new world of reality. . . . She rose free on the wings of her new condition" (400). Ursula thus consigns Gudrun to a metaphoric abyss with all the rest of the past; the next scene literalizes the metaphor through placing Gudrun in an actual abyss, longing to be in yet another. This concrete realization of Ursula's metaphor implies the following distinction: Ursula's "heart of reality" is the ideal or metaphysical or even mystical goal of human relationship while Gudrun's "heart of the frozen, mysterious navel of the world" is no more than an actual site of isolation and alienation.

Yet the verbal similarities in these two passages force us to see the experiences of Gudrun and Ursula in terms of each other. We are prevented from any simple evaluation of either experience, for the polarity in meanings for terms like "oneness" and "heart" and "oblivion" produces finally an ambiguity that provokes us to wonder about the extent to which Ursula's "oneness with Birkin" represents a withdrawal from life and the extent to which Gudrun's passionate desire for "oneness" with "the All" contains life-giving potential. This last question may arise especially insistently given the repetitions of "navel" in the passage concerning Gudrun. The image of the "infolded navel" evokes the bud imagery poignantly associated with Gudrun's failed hopes: "'Don't you find, that things fail to materialise?'" she asks Ursula at the beginning of the novel. "'*Nothing materialises!* Everything withers in the bud'" (2). The organic metaphor prevents us from entirely dissociating Gudrun from the possibility of growth and makes all the more distressing the rigidification of her soul as symbolized by the flowerlike peaks of the frozen Alps.

One of the most disquieting qualities of *Women in Love* is that apparent oppositions are couched in terminology that has an essential "sameness" about it. So, for example, some key terms like "inhuman," "pure," "perfect," and "mystic" are used to present both Gerald's worship of the machine and a moment of transcendent sexual experience shared by Birkin and Ursula. What is one to make of the recognition that a kind of inhuman purity of being is both Birkin's goal in his relationship with Ursula and Gerald's goal for the organization of his business?[2] On the one hand, we think that we clearly see the difference. We know that there are vital and deathly forms of worship in *Women in Love,* vital and deathly modes of consciousness, feeling, and speaking. There are virtues and the simulacra of virtues. And we have no trouble distinguishing the "saved" from the "damned," or to use Leo Bersani's terminology, the "life-seekers" from the "death-seekers" (182), even if we are as sensitive as Bersani to the way in which the language of the novel blurs apparently important distinctions.

Yet on the other hand, the established polarities or oppositions tend to collapse or dissolve when we start looking at the language closely, so that what we actually have is a series of meanings that shade into each other, a series with extremes or poles that become associated with, if not transformed into, each other. Colin Clarke's study of "dissolution" in romantic poetry and in Lawrence illustrates this principle when Clarke shows the "tendency of images of dissolution to polarise, pointing to possibilities both of disembodiment and decay, ecstasy and reduction" (28). I am suggesting that Clarke's conclusions with regard to images of lapsing, falling, streaming, and dissolving apply more generally to the language of *Women in Love,* that it is true with many key terms, to use Clarke's words, that the occurrences of the term "are so deviously and closely related in the novel's shifting linguistic contexts that any given use . . . is likely to entail the others, if only in a shadowy way"; the result is "that every usage is charged with either concealed or manifest tension" (Clarke 41). To say this is to suggest that J. Hillis Miller's remark with regard to words with the double antithetical prefix "para" is more generally applicable to the language of Lawrence's novel: "Though a given word ... may seem to choose univocally one of these possibilities [of meaning], the other meanings are always there as a shimmering in the word which makes it refuse to stay still in the sentence" ("The Critic as Host" 219).

Go, Going, Gone: A Linguistic Journey into the Abyss

That images of dissolution and the figure of the abyss are not oddities in this regard, not isolated examples of a peculiar linguistic pattern, can be seen by tracing the use of the term *go* in the novel. A common term, seemingly a literal one, *go* is nonetheless particularly resonant in this text because of the multiplicity of meanings that it acquires. Surprisingly often it is used figuratively, and its figurative uses seem to define the possibilities of action open to the characters in the novel. Indeed, the term returns us to my initial assertion, that the action of *Women in Love* is generated by the figure of a confrontation with an abyss or void. Confronted with an abyss, one either keeps going in some way or stops going, and the text progressively literalizes in specific actions meanings introduced by metaphoric uses of *go*.

Even the earliest occurrences of the term are portentous. As the Brangwen sisters walk through Beldover on the way to the Crich wedding, Gudrun is depressed by the sordidness of the town and intimidated by the staring wives of the colliers: "all the time her heart was crying, as if in the midst of some ordeal: "'I want to go back, I want to go away, I want not to know it, not to know that this exists.' Yet she must go forward" (6). Confronted by the staring crowd at the church, she cries "'Let us go back.... But must we go through them?'" (7). Through these repetitions of the verb *go,* it is as if the novel is telling the possibilities of action or movement open to Gudrun in the face of the void, that "terrifying chasm," each of those possibilities already bearing for this member of the "damned" a sinister connotation.

But perhaps the most sinister implication of *go* is established by a punning conversation between the two sisters in "Diver." They speak of Gerald:

> "He is several generations of youngness at one go. They hate him for it. He takes them all by the scruff of the neck, and fairly flings them along. He'll have to die soon, when he's made every possible improvement, and there will be nothing more to improve. He's got *go,* anyhow."
>
> "Certainly he's got go," said Gudrun. "In fact I've never seen a man that showed signs of so much. The unfortunate thing is, where does his *go* go to, what becomes of it?"
>
> "Oh, I know," said Ursula. "It goes in applying the latest appliances!"
>
> "Exactly!" said Gudrun.
>
> "You know he shot his brother?" said Ursula. (53)

Gerald's shooting of his brother is the logical outcome of his "go"—of his compulsion to apply appliances. The passage thus insinuates the self-destructive potential of Gerald's "go," with Gudrun's question, "where does his *go* go to," implying the possibility of exhaustion and reinforcing Ursula's suggestion that the logical end of Gerald's activity is death.

On the other hand, *go* reverberates with creative possibility in "Excurse," where going is movement—desirable movement—into the unknown. When Ursula asks Birkin, "And where are we going?" he gives her "the answer she liked": " 'Anywhere' " (295). He tells her : " 'I should like to go with you—nowhere. . . . One wants to wander away from the world's somewheres, into our own nowhere' " (307–8). Here, *go* encompasses a metaphorical journey to a metaphorical place, " 'somewhere where [they] can be free,' " not " 'a locality though' ": " 'It's a perfected relation,' " Birkin insists (308). The rest of the chapter gives substance to these metaphors. They drive into Sherwood Forest and stop at a dark, silent place where "the world was under a strange ban" (312)—that is, at a place not to be perceived as a place, a "nowhere." In this nonplace, the language of the passage insists, they achieve a transcendent, liberating union.

The example of "Excurse" is part of a larger-scale realization of the metaphor of a journey. With respect to Ursula and Birkin, the variations of this metaphor—and the variations upon the motif of "going"—can be summarized as follows. In "An Island" (ch. 9), they row to an island across Willey Water, an action foreshadowing that longer journey away from civilization and toward isolation that is the scheme of their relationship in the novel. In "Mino" (ch. 13), Birkin's speeches contain an implicit metaphor of a journey into the unknown: " 'I deliver *myself* over to the unknown, in coming to you . . . ' " (138). The pun on delivery is repeated in the next chapter, "Water-Party," where Birkin speaks of wanting " 'love that is like sleep, like being born again' " (178), a deathlike state, a being "gone" that precedes delivery into a new life and a new world: " 'One is delivered over like a naked infant from the womb . . . ' " (178). This is birth as exploratory journey, exploration of the abyss as fecund void; yet this going into the unknown is also a going away from oneself, an attempt to escape self-consciousness: " 'I want to be gone out of myself, and you to be lost to yourself, so we are found different' " (179). The motive of escape recurs in Ursula's meditation on death as a journey into the unknown, at the beginning of the next chapter, "Sunday Evening." In "Moony" (ch. 19), when Birkin meditates upon the various "ways" or directions that the development of an individual or a race can take, there are three versions of the journey into the unknown: the African process, where the soul after a death-break, will "travel" or "lapse" toward "purely sensual understanding, knowledge in the mystery of dissolution" (246); the Arctic process, where the soul of the white races, "having the arctic north behind them," travels toward "snow-abstract annihilation" (246); and the "way of freedom"—a "paradisal entry into pure single being" (247).

Thus, before "Excurse," the metaphor of a journey appears in a number of different forms. "Excurse" itself is a pivotal chapter in which the metaphor is transformed into a concrete experience—the auto trip into Sherwood Forest. After "Excurse" the novel continues to literalize the metaphor with respect to Ursula and Birkin; that is, the novel focuses on their physical movements from England to the Tyrol to Italy to the Tyrol to England again. The metaphor of a journey is repeatedly transvalued, and the travels that literalize that metaphor are of equivocal meaning. Ceaseless journeying in a world that is round and does not run off into space (as Birkin sometimes wishes he could do) is bound eventually to take on the appearance of travelling in circles. When Birkin returns to the Tyrol to claim Gerald's body, he seems to perceive that the distinction between the kinds of motion is difficult to maintain; he questions his transitory mode of existence and the ideal of perpetual journeying: "Was it a way out? It was only a way in again" (469). And the final, brief scene of the novel, which pictures Birkin and Ursula back at the Mill (the home that Birkin left behind when they embarked upon their journey), constitutes an implicit reconsideration of the ideal of mobility.

But it is not merely this circular pattern in their travels that urges us to question the value of journeying. To the extent that the motif depends upon repetitions of the term *go,* the notion of Gerald's "go" lurks in the background of the word, provoking us to ask what Birkin's wanderlust may have in common with Gerald's compulsive movements, his subjection to the rotary motion of the machine. Gerald's progress through the novel realizes concretely the quite evidently implied answer to Gudrun's question, " 'where does his *go* go to?' " Gerald's "go" is exhaustible: it goes away, it leads to death. Toiling up the Alpine slopes for the last time, he only wants "to go on, to go on whilst he could, to move, to keep going, that was all, to keep going, until it was finished" (465).

Multiple senses of *go* are given actuality by Gerald's experiences. On the other side of his "go," his self-defeating improving and organizing, is a need to "let go." Early on, Birkin sees that Gerald is doomed by his inability to "fly away from himself" (199); and in "The Industrial Magnate," partially awaking from "a sort of trance of activity" (224) that has constituted his life for years, Gerald knows that "there was no equilibrium [for him]. He would have to go in some direction, shortly, to find relief" (225). Although the direction that he finally takes—indeed seems compelled to take—is toward death, "letting go" itself has positive and negative connotations. In "Gladiatorial," Birkin suggests wrestling as a cure for Gerald's complaint, " 'I can't apply myself' " (359). The wrestling leaves Gerald momentarily inert but seems to generate his sudden clasp of Birkin's hand, that "warm, momentaneous grip of final love"

(471) which Birkin remembers after Gerald's death. This brief hour of letting go, which suggests the possibility of authentic relationship between Birkin and Gerald, contrasts with another kind of abandon toward which Gerald's desires lead him, an abandon that implies the breaking of all bonds. In "Threshold," both he and Gudrun feel "the subterranean desire to let go, to fling away everything, and lapse into sheer unrestraint, brutal and licentious" (279). "Letting go" thus embraces the creative and destructive possibilities of releasing what is "unknown and suppressed" (280) in the individual.

"Going" and "letting go" are keys to the structure of "Death and Love." Like "Excurse," which directly precedes it and with which it is paired as a central consummation in the novel, this chapter literalizes in the second half verbal formulations or metaphors that occur in the first half. The chapter is organized around two walks across the countryside, each one culminating in a scene of sexual passion; and the chapter is bifurcated by the death of Mr. Crich—death being another kind of "going" in *Women in Love*. In the first half of the chapter, letting go is identified with collapse. Gerald confesses to Gudrun his sense of "'universal collapse'" impending within himself: "'You know that sooner or later you'll *have* to let go'" (317), he says with reference to himself. Gudrun's physical presence here seems to pull him back from the edge of the abyss over which he feels suspended. But his respite—his sense of equilibrium and strength during their walk early in the chapter—is temporary, for after his father's death (also presented in terms of going—"he's gone," the members of the Crich family keep saying), "He did not believe in his own strength any more. He could not fall into this infinite void and rise again. . . . He must withdraw, he must seek reinforcements. He did not believe in his own single self any further than this" (330). At this point, going and letting go become equivalent. Gerald stumbles across the countryside ("Where was he going? No matter" [330]) ending his journey in Gudrun's bedroom.

"Death and Love," like its structural counterpart "Excurse," is a pivotal chapter. After "Death and Love," letting go depends upon going away, upon travel, for Gerald and Gudrun. At dinner in Basle Gudrun asserts, "'It is quite impossible really to let go, in England, of that I am assured'" (385). In two long chapters set in the Tyrol, physical activity is the form that letting go takes. Arriving in the Tyrol, Gerald and Gudrun feel "powerful enough to leap over the confines of life into the forbidden places, and back again" (389). Literalized, this potentially freeing leap becomes "an ecstasy of physical motion, sleighing, ski-ing, skating, moving in an intensity of speed and white light that surpassed life itself, and carried the souls of the human beings beyond into an inhuman abstraction of velocity and weight and eternal, frozen snow" (411). The abandon here implies no life-giving release of energy, but rather moves in the direction of "snow-abstract annihilation."

This last phrase occurs in "Moony" as Birkin thinks, "The white races, having the Arctic north behind them, the vast abstraction of ice and snow, would fulfil a mystery of ice-destructive knowledge, snow-abstract annihilation" (246). In "Continental," Gerald's trajectory coincides with the one that Birkin imagines in "Moony": "Gerald's eyes became hard and strange, and as he went by on his skis he was more like some powerful, fateful sigh than a man, his muscles elastic in a perfect soaring trajectory, his body projected in pure flight, mindless, soulless, whirling along one perfect line of force" (411–12). No longer "like a machine that is without power" (258), Gerald is still machinelike: "Gerald worked perfectly.... It seemed to him the flying sledge was but his own strength spread out...the motion was but his own" (411). Gudrun now thinks of Gerald as "an instrument": "He only needed to be hitched on, he needed that his hand should be set to the task..." (407). A kind of literalization goes on here: earlier in the novel the metaphor of a machine has as its tenor Gerald's inner workings; now it comes concretely to describe his physical mode of existence as well.

The only fulfilment for a machine is in going. The "ecstasy of physical motion" in "Continental," an ecstasy in which all four major characters participate, reaches a climax with a toboggan ride which Gudrun describes as the most "complete moment" of her life (411) and with Gerald's "pure flight...along one perfect line of force" (412). Then an abrupt shift in the narrative tempo and the intensity of the language signals that the limits of their activity have been reached: "Luckily there came a day of snow when they must all stay indoors: otherwise, Birkin said, they would all lose their faculties, and begin to utter themselves in cries and shrieks, like some strange, unknown species of snow-creatures" (412). Intensities of motion become the object of contemplation through Loerke's description of his freize: "It was a representation of a fair, with peasants and artisans in an orgy of enjoyment, drunk and absurd in their modern dress, whirling ridiculously in roundabouts, gaping at shows, kissing and staggering and rolling in knots, swinging in swing-boats, and firing down shooting galleries, a frenzy of chaotic motion" (414). The plot implicitly comments on the limitations of such fulfilment when Birkin and Ursula decide to leave.

After their departure, considerations of going almost form a litany: " 'In the end...I shall go away from him' " (436); " 'Where shall I go?' " (437); "He would not go away from her whatever she said or did" (437); " 'Go away,' she cried, 'and leave me to it' " (438); "The climax of sensual reaction, once reached in any direction, is reached finally, there is no going on" (443); " 'I shall not go back to England.... I can't see the use of going back' " (452); " 'I will go away...' " (454); " 'We will go together as far as Innsbruck, for appearance's sake?' " (459); " 'You are going away tomorrow?' " (461); "He only wanted to go on, to go on whilst he could, to move, to keep going, that was all, to keep going, until it was finished" (465). This recitation reminds us that like Ursula and Birkin, Gudrun and Gerald move toward the unknown, although they finally embark upon separate journeys. "Snowed Up" posits nullity or death as the alternative to going away:

> Sometimes it was he who seemed strongest, whilst she was almost gone, creeping near the earth like a spent wind; sometimes it was the reverse. But always it was this eternal see-saw, one destroyed that the other might exist, one ratified because the other was nulled.
> "In the end," she said to herself, "I shall go away from him."
> "I can be free of her," he said to himself in his paroxysms of suffering. (436)

The rest of the novel realizes the different but interdependent senses of the passive infinitive "to be gone" implicitly defined here: flight and death.

Obviously Gerald's death in the snow literalizes both senses at the same time that it realizes the process of "snow-abstract annihilation." Gudrun, in the final chapters, progressively becomes "gone" as her experiences realize in a peculiar way "the long, long African process of purely sensual understanding, knowledge in the mystery of dissolution" (246). Birkin's ruminations in "Moony" provide a paradigm for Gudrun's experiences in "Continental" and "Snowed Up":

> There is a long way we can travel after the death-break: after that point when the soul in intense suffering breaks, breaks away from its organic hold like a leaf that falls. We fall from the connection with life and hope, we lapse from pure integral being, from creation and liberty, and we fall into the long, long African process.... (246)

The imagery of later chapters progressively suggests that Gudrun enacts such a "death of the creative spirit." This enactment begins upon her arrival in the Tyrol, where the landscape

> filled Gudrun with a strange rapture. She crouched in front of the window, clenching her face in her hands, in a sort of trance. At last she had arrived, she had reached her place. Here at least she folded her venture and settled down like a crystal in the navel of snow and was gone.
> Gerald bent above her and was looking out over her shoulder. Already he felt she was alone. She was gone. She was completely gone, and there was an icy vapour round his heart. (391)

Gudrun is "gone" not only in the sense of being transported by the landscape, but also in the sense of having broken away from life, of having reached "that point where the soul in intense suffering breaks, breaks away from its organic hold like a leaf that falls": she "settled down like a crystal."

The rigidification of the organic metaphors in the final section of the novel signifies such a break. In the first chapter of *Women in Love,* Gudrun complains, "'*Nothing materialises*! Everything withers in the bud'" (2); in the closing chapters, the frozen beauty of the landscape, in the form of flowerlike mountain peaks, presents the materialization indeed of life's promise for Gudrun: "in the heaven the peaks of snow were rosy, glistening like transcendent, radiant spikes of blossom in the heavenly upper-world, so lovely and beyond" (392). Gudrun's worship of the flowering landscape represents isolation and a kind of emotional death, as is clear from the juxtaposition of two different uses of the organic metaphor in "Snowed Up." One use hints at the potentialities of Gerald and Gudrun: he feels like "a seed that has germinated, to issue forth in being" (437) and she feels "as if he tore at the bud of her heart. . . . [H]e would destroy her as an immature bud, torn open, is destroyed" (437). The promise implied by such images is foreclosed in the scene where Gudrun worships the Alpine landscape:

> Then in the east the peaks and ridges glowed with living rose, incandescent like immortal flowers against a purple-brown sky, a miracle, whilst down below the world was a bluish shadow, and above, like an annunciation, hovered a rosy transport in mid-air.
>   To her it was so beautiful, it was a delirium, she wanted to gather the glowing, eternal peaks to her breast, and die. (438)

Not only does Gudrun check the flowering of her soul, she worships its unattainability as it is represented in the form of apparently endless flowerlike peaks beyond her. Her transport here is the ultimate in self-abandon. And when Gudrun rejects him in this scene, Gerald's yearning—"the quickening, the going forth in him"—turns upon itself and is transformed into the most sinister of promises: " 'In the end,' he said to himself with real voluptuous promise '. . . I shall do away with her' " (438–39). The change in the tenor of the flower metaphor, from the creative human soul to the frozen Alpine landscape, signifies ultimate spiritual recoil in both Gudrun and Gerald.

The Abyss of Language

One implication of this discussion of literalization is that *Women in Love* makes a covert attempt to answer Gudrun's question, " 'What is it all but words!' " (4). Gudrun is thinking of the metaphor of an abyss or chasm implied by her own talk of taking a jump over an edge, a metaphor I have called the initiatory figure of the novel. In the sense that action and setting seem to issue from Gudrun's words, her question commands an ironic reading: What indeed? one might respond. For the progressive literalization of some of the metaphors of the novel implicitly argues that words do have substance, that they can take us somewhere, that they can transport us to reality or actuality.

Women in Love in fact explicitly concerns itself with these possibilities, most explicitly in "Water-Party" where Birkin confuses Ursula by switching metaphors midspeech:

There was always confusion in speech. Yet it must be spoken. Which ever way one moved, if one were to move forwards, one must break a way through. And to know, to give utterance, was to break a way through the walls of the prison as the infant in labour strives through the walls of the womb. There is no new movement now, without the breaking through of the old body, deliberately, in knowledge, in the struggle to get out. (178–79)

One important assumption here is that language can move us in a positive direction—toward freedom, toward "birth."[3] At the same time, however, the passage contains a movement that may cause us to question this assumption. A peculiar kind of permutation occurs: the metaphor of breaking a way out of prison is repeated by a kind of superimposition upon or elision with the metaphor of birth so that we read that the infant, not the mother, is "in labour," striving "through the walls of the womb" rather than being expelled by them. This figure, in turn, is transformed into one that calls to mind a snake's shedding of its skin, yet the figure of "the breaking through of the old body" does not exactly correspond to this process either, nor to anything else I can think of. Such sequences of metaphors constitute "the continual, slightly modified repetition" which, Lawrence insists in the foreword to the novel, is a "natural" feature of his style; they are his attempts to give names to the unnamed, to give substance to the insubstantial. Yet clearly the displacements of metaphors in such passages could continue indefinitely. Thus, if the passage argues that words can take us somewhere, it also forces us to ask where they take us.

As was the case in *The Rainbow,* literalization may be read as an affirmation of the symbolic conception of the sign and as a kind of logocentric impulse in the novel, as a reaching toward some actuality to which words refer. But the very process of tracing this movement exposes the insubstantiality of words and the instability of meaning. The multiform occurrences of "to go" and of associated metaphors and symbols reflect upon each other in such a way as to dramatize the self-questioning and self-subversive energies of language. It is in fact perfectly characteristic of the language of *Women in Love* that the motif of going, in its multiple senses, finds its fulfilment in images of stasis: in the Birkins' sojourn at the Mill, in Gudrun's identification with "the sleeping, timeless, frozen centre of all," and in Gerald's death by freezing. It is equally characteristic of the novel that the terminology of stasis illustrates the same point. Stillness or stasis can encompass almost diametrically opposed meanings in *Women in Love,* both the inertia from which Gerald suffers and the transcendent peace that Birkin experiences from time to time with Ursula. Yet each of these meanings in turn involves a kind of paradox, for Gerald's inertia takes the form of constant restlessness while Birkin's moments of undesiring stillness occur while he is in transit (for example, as he crosses the English Channel).

The double interrogative movement represented by the terminology of going and staying is not the only means by which the novel illustrates the self-reflexive energies of language. Such energies are also evident in the interplay between literal and figurative uses of a single word or related terms. A good example is the terminology of balance, suspension, and equilibrium—terminology closely allied to the figure of an abyss. We assume that Birkin is on the brink of attaining the star-equilibrium to which some of his earlier speeches refer when in "Excurse" we read that he "would be night-free, like an Egyptian, steadfast in perfect suspended equilibrium, pure mystic nodality of physical being" (311–12) and that he and Ursula "would give each other this star-equilibrium which alone is freedom" (312). We can see that the metaphors point toward that sense of wholeness and perfected being that he seeks through his relationship with Ursula.

Gerald desires but fails to find such a sense, a failure that appears to be reflected in the next chapter, "Death and Love," by the "degeneration" or "decline" of the metaphor of equilibrium into the literal use of the term "balance"; Gudrun "was drawn against him as they walked down the stormy darkness. He seemed to balance her perfectly in opposition to himself, in their dual motion of walking. So, suddenly, he was liberated and perfect, strong, heroic" (321). The shift from the metaphoric to the literal invites us to see Gerald's liberation and strength as a parody of Birkin's state in the preceding chapter. And indeed, Gerald's sense is purely temporary: within a few pages, in a new scene, he is "suspended on the edge of a void, writhing" (330).

Now Gerald's metaphorical suspension here is obviously quite different from Birkin's "perfectly suspended equilibrium," yet this repetition with variation is but one more example of the self-subverting quality of the language of *Women in Love,* for it threatens to collapse the very opposition it seeks to establish. Beyond this, the intensity of the language in the description of Gerald's state of suspension is important to notice:

> And all the time he was like a man hung in chains over the edge of an abyss.... [F]riends or strangers, or work or play... it all showed him only the same bottomless void, in which his heart swung perishing. There was no escape, there was nothing to grasp hold of. He must writhe on the edge of the chasm, suspended in chains of invisible physical life. (330)

After this, one could scarcely fail to notice the repetition of the motif of suspension a few pages later in the scene where Gerald is sneaking into the Brangwen house in order to seek out Gudrun in bed. There Gerald "suspends" his movements in order not to awaken the family: "Gerald stood a second suspended. He glanced down the passage behind him. It was all dark. Again he was suspended. Then he went swiftly upstairs" (333). This shift in the use of the metaphor—this movement from something that sounds like cosmic suffering to something that sounds like a case of "nerves"—is practically bathetic.

Such effects should remind us that "abyss" and "bathos" have the same Greek root (*buthos*) and that the narrative generated by the figure of the abyss is offered up in *Women in Love* by words that through their own movements suggest what we might mean in speaking of the abyss of language. The interplay of figurative and literal produces the effect of "sinking" that I have mentioned, and the tendency, with many terms, for meanings to proliferate then polarize may create in the reader a sense of never getting to the "bottom" of meaning in *Women in Love.*[4]

Women in Love: Repetition and the Differential Metaphysic

One does hit bottom in reading this novel. Even as the text blurs the distinction between apparent oppositions, it establishes a firm ground of difference against which the similarities manifest themselves and in the context of which they may be further discriminated. Verbal repetition in *Women in Love* becomes the means by which the novel makes the reader aware of the differential nature of language, of the contextuality of words.[1] Such repetition has a structural analogue in episodic repetition, the recurrence of certain types of action or scene: just as the same word can have almost opposite meanings in different contexts, so can similar actions by different characters in different contexts. Ultimately, as I shall argue, verbal and episodic repetition are the means by which the novel tests a differential model of the self.[2]

A World of Difference

Difference—human difference at least—is a matter of concern to the characters in Lawrence's novel, and the range of assertion on this subject is represented by two different statements made by Birkin. In the earlier of the two, he rises to counter Hermione's claim that people are "all equal in the spirit":

> "It is just the opposite, just the contrary, Hermione. We are all different and unequal in spirit—it is only the *social* differences that are based on accidental material conditions. We are all abstractly or mathematically equal, if you like. Every man has hunger and thirst, two eyes, one nose and two legs. We're all the same in point of hunger. But spiritually there is pure difference and neither equality or inequality counts." (96)

Pure difference is Birkin's name for the intrinsic otherness of human beings from one another, for what constitutes the "real impersonal me, that is beyond love, beyond any emotional relationship" (137), the "final" and "inhuman" self beyond personality—and "beyond responsibility" (137)—of which Birkin speaks so extensively in "Mino." Though "pure difference" may have the sound of a differential concept, it actually is central to a logocentric-organic concept of the self, that is, to a concept that posits a core of essential, unique being—"intrinsic otherness"—in the individual. That this is the case becomes plainer as Birkin complains, in "Excurse," about the lack of such "stark unknown" being in others

> [Birkin] was not very much interested any more in personalities and in people—people were all different, but they were all enclosed nowadays in a definite limitation, he said; there were only about two great ideas, two great streams of activity remaining, with various forms of reaction therefrom. The reactions were all varied in various people, but they followed a few great laws, and intrinsically there was no difference. They acted and reacted involuntarily according to a few great laws, and once the laws, the great principles, were known, people were no longer mystically interesting. They were all essentially alike, the differences were only variations on a theme. None of them transcended the given terms. (296–97)

Intrinsically there was no difference: somewhat paradoxically one could say that there is only a superficial difference between this statement and Saussure's claim for the differential nature of language: "in language there are only differences *without positive terms*" (120). For it is by superficial or extrinsic differences alone—social differences and differences at the level of observable behavior or "personality"—that one person is distinguished from another; there *is* no *intrinsic otherness*.

There is indeed nothing intrinsic—no positive term or presence—so Birkin seems to be saying. Even of "the two great streams of activity," the "few great laws," the passage seems to assert that "intrinsically there was no difference." As if to stress the point that opposites somehow are always the same, Birkin exclaims to Ursula, in response to her disdain for Hermione, " 'to be her opposite is to be her counterpart' " (297). No one transcends "the given terms," a linguistic metaphor that confirms the appropriateness of the analogy with language in discussing the means by which identity emerges; people are "essentially alike" in being constituted only by their *extrinsic* differences.

Such a reading of the passage poses the question of whether Birkin can legitimately speak of *intrinsic difference* or *pure difference* or whether indeed he can properly speak of the *intrinsic* at all. It is precisely such questions, I am claiming, that the novel as a whole (like *The Rainbow* before it) explores. Birkin's insistence on the possibility of a self, a "final me," that is "stark and impersonal and beyond responsibility" (137) affirms the possibility of a nonrelational, nonreactive ("beyond responsibility") self, a self anterior to consciousness and commitment; and the narrative of *Women in Love* endorses this possibility through the imagery of golden light and the terminology of pure presence pervading the consummation scene at the end of "Excurse." But not only is it the case that the scene, situated as it is near the center of the novel, does not provide us with "the last word" on being in the novel; it is ironic and telling that the powerful organic-logocentric rhetoric, the rhetoric of presence, emerges precisely at the point where the narrative makes plainest the dependence of the "real self" on responsiveness to the other.

Everything worth saying either in favor of or against the language at the end of "Excurse" has probably already been said; a further point worth making is that Lawrence does not rely purely upon the language *within* the passage to convey the quality of the experience he is presenting. It is by means of its *difference* from the language of an analogous passage in the next chapter, "Death and Love," that "Excurse" conveys the uniqueness, the singularity, of the experience Birkin and Ursula share.[3] Both passages present scenes of sexual passion in language that relies heavily upon forms of *know*, upon words possessing negative prefixes or suffixes ("inhuman," "unthinkable," "unutterable," "unspeakable," "untranslatable," and "mindlessly"), and upon words that have the force of absolutes or superlatives ("perfect," "pure," "supreme").

In "Excurse," the complex of terms related to knowledge defines a paradoxical kind of knowledge earned by Birkin and Ursula, "the knowledge which is death of knowledge" (311), but it is the contrasting use of similar terminology in "Death and Love" that makes it plain that this "unthinkable" unknowing knowledge in "Excurse" is no mere mindless (in the ordinary sense) submersion in the senses. Such submersion is what we find in "Death and Love," where degree words and quantifiers ("so," "such," "how much more," "too," "all," "enough") and an emphasis on physical action all point to a knowledge neither abstruse nor paradoxical. The knowledge Gudrun seeks is an accumulation of sensations:

> She reached up, like Eve reaching to the apples on the tree of knowledge, and she kissed him, though her passion was a transcendent fear of the thing he was, touching his face with her infinitely delicate, encroaching, wondering fingers.... How much more of him was there for her to know? Ah, much, much, many days harvesting.... (324)

Even the shape of some of the sentences defines Gudrun's knowledge here as a collection of discrete sensations (like little apples she gathers from the tree of sensuous knowledge): "She kissed him, putting her fingers over his eyes, his nostrils, over his brows and ears, to his neck, to know him, to gather him in by touch" (324). While syntactic repetitions ("She wanted to touch him and touch him and touch him" [324]) insinuate Gudrun's compulsive need to touch, the stress in "Excurse," where "touch" is also an important word, is on the connection established through touch: "Darkness and silence must fall perfectly upon her, then she could know mystically, in unrevealed touch. She must lightly, mindlessly connect with him, have the knowledge which is death of knowledge, the reality of surety in not-knowing" (311). The intransitive use of *know* and the repudiative phrases "death of knowledge" and "not-knowing" clearly distinguish Ursula's experience from any form of mental consciousness, from any form of "transitive" knowing.

One might say then that there are no positive terms by which Birkin and Ursula's experience may be presented. Rather the experience is defined only in terms of what it is not: first by the negative word formations within the passage, and then by the contrasts provided by the rhetoric of the passage in "Death and Love." The powerful affirmation of being as presence at the end of "Excurse"—"the immemorial magnificence of mystic, palpable, real otherness" (312)—is, then, compromised by the differential dynamics of the text.

Context and the Dynamics of Linguistic Difference

Those dynamics so thoroughly characterize the text that even apparently empty intensifiers like "really" participate in them. Both the characters and the narrator of *Women in Love* display a predilection for adverbs of degree and manner, as is apparent even in the opening pages of the novel. There Lawrence's care to render the minutiae of physical and emotional attitude accounts for a proliferation of such adverbs: "mostly," "slightly," "ironically," coolly," "angrily." At the same time, adverbs of degree abound as intensifiers in the speech of some of the characters:

> "Oh my dear," cried Gudrun strident, "I wouldn't go out of my way to look for him [a man to marry]. But if there did happen to come along a *highly* attractive individual of sufficient means—well—" she tailed off *ironically*. Then she looked *searchingly* at Ursula, as if to probe her....
> "Of course there's children—" said Ursula *doubtfully*.
> Gudrun's face hardened.
> "Do you *really* want children, Ursula?" she asked *coldly*. (2–3, emphasis added except for that of *really*)

Such passages provoke the suspicion that everything predicated of the characters must be qualified or modified, everything asserted by them, intensified. When so many -ly adverbs occur in close succession they may strike the reader almost as a mechanical tic of style,[4] but in actuality this kind of verbal repetition serves a process of differentiation.

Words like "really" really do constitute a verbal tic in the speech of some of the characters:

"You wouldn't consider a good offer?" asked Gudrun.

"I think I've rejected several," said Ursula.

"Really!" Gudrun flushed dark—"But anything really worthwhile? Have you *really?*"

"A thousand a year, and an awfully nice man. I liked him awfully," said Ursula.

"Really! But weren't you fearfully tempted?" (2)

That Gudrun uses "really" seven times in the first three pages of the book gives us grounds for connecting her with the vapid and depraved Pussum, who grills Gerald about his experience in the Amazon thus:

"Were you ever *vewy* much afwaid of the savages?" she asked in her calm, dull, childish voice.

"No—never very much afraid. On the whole they're harmless—they're not born yet, you can't feel really afraid of them. You know you can manage them."

"Do you *weally?* Aren't they *vewy* fierce?"

"Not very. There aren't many fierce things, as a matter of fact...."

"Except in herds," interrupted Birkin.

"Aren't there *weally?*" she said. (59, emphasis added)

And Hermione's "so" is the counterpart of Gudrun's "really" and Pussum's "weally" and "vewy":

"Well—" rumbled Hermione. "I don't know. To me the pleasure of knowing is *so* great, *so* wonderful—nothing has meant so much to me in all life, as certain knowledge—no, I am sure—nothing."

"What knowledge, for example, Hermione?" asked Alexander.

Hermione lifted her face and rumbled—"M-m-m-I don't know.... But one thing was the stars, when I really understood something about the stars. One feels so *uplifted,* so *unbounded....*" (78, ellipsis marks in text)

Such intensifiers which, in the speech of certain characters, substitute both for substance and genuine intensity or dynamism, recur in the narrative; but even where they do little more than convey extremity of emotion or perception, they are rarely coy or overinsistent as they are in the speeches I have quoted. More important, the narrative of *Women in Love* often "recovers" for such terms meanings lost in dialogue.

In the first chapter, for instance, Ursula mentions a proposal she has had from an "'awfully nice'" man; Gudrun wonders that her sister was not "'fearfully tempted.'" The adverbs are mannerisms, and there is only an ironic gap between the emptiness of their references to fear and the actual, unacknowledged fears that the sisters both feel in this scene. But later when Ursula sees Birkin before her "so awfully real, that her heart almost stopped beating" (306), the relative clause insists upon the meaning—the meaningfulness—of "awfully." The case is similar in "Crème de Menthe," where Gerald feels "an awful, enjoyable power" over the Pussum, "an instinctive cherishing very near to cruelty" (57). And "dreadfully" undergoes similar permutations: Hermione is " 'dreadfully sorry' " (136) when she drops Gudrun's sketchbook in the pond; her obsession with knowledge, however, is truly "a dreadful tyranny . . . in her" (100).

It is such differences or, for another example, the difference between Hermione's exclaiming that she feels " 'so unbounded' " and her creator's writing as straightforward description that Ursula possessed Birkin "so utterly and intolerably that she herself lapsed out" (361) that enable the reader to distinguish between the inauthentic and authentic modes of experience in *Women in Love*. The language in which Ursula's experience is rendered resolutely indicates that a boundary *has* been crossed, an outer limit transgressed; the relative clause, "that she herself lapsed out," thus affirms the meaning of "utterly" in its root sense. The dramatic context of Hermione's exclamation, on the other hand, reveals the emptiness of her words. Birkin perceives the irony that it is " 'certain knowledge' " that makes her feel " 'so *unbounded*' " and retorts, " 'What do you want to feel unbounded for? . . . You don't want to *be* unbounded' " (96).

The Differential Dance of *Love*

Such differences are further established in the dialogue of *Women in Love* through the repetitions of that term of central thematic import, *love*. Michael Ragussis has claimed that "over the course of the novel, new meanings are given to 'love' . . . by Birkin's conversations with the other characters" (183). And certainly there is a sense in which this term, which most often—and tellingly—occurs in contexts of hatred and hostility, is redeemed or revitalized through the relation, especially through the dialogue, of Ursula and Birkin. But as important as *love*'s meaning—or meaningfulness—are the differential uses to which Lawrence puts its movements through the text.

In "An Island" (ch. 11), Birkin says of *love*: " 'The point about love . . . is that we hate the word because we have vulgarised it. It ought to be . . . tabooed from utterance, for many years, till we get a new, better idea' " (22). Birkin's complaint is that *love* has become no more than a mask for hate: " 'Look at all the millions of people who repeat every minute that love is the greatest . . . and see what they are doing all the time. By their works ye shall know them for dirty liars and cowards. . . . You might as well say that hate is the greatest . . . ' " (119). The abuse of the word to which Birkin refers can, in the novel, be associated with a belief in absolute or static meaning or a refusal to see the contextuality of words. Because this belief can be allied with the symbolic model of language, the abuse of *love* implicitly questions that model at the same time that it exposes the emotional and moral limitations of the characters.

The importance of these associations is plainly dramatized in "The Industrial Magnate," where the abuse of the word *love* provides an important analogue to larger misuses of power. One great irony in the career of Thomas Crich is that although love is central to his conception of himself—"He had been so constant to his lights, so constant to charity, and to his love for his neighbour" (207)—his marriage proves to be "a relation of utter interdestruction" (209). It is not Crich's marriage, however, but his recognition of "a state of war" with his miners that breaks his heart by destroying his illusion that his business is "run on love" (217):

> Seething masses of miners met daily, carried away by a new religious impulse. The idea flew through them: "All men are equal on earth," and they would carry the idea to its material fulfillment. After all, is it not the teaching of Christ? And what is an idea if not the germ of action in the material world.... It was a religious creed pushed to its material conclusion.... Even in the machine, there should be equality.... [T]he desire for chaos had risen, and the idea of mechanical equality was the weapon of disruption which should execute the will of man, the will for chaos. (217-19)

The miners' efforts to find a material equivalent for a spiritual concept are no more successful than are Ursula's adolescent efforts to "possess" Christ in physical terms. The failure of the miners' efforts underscores the incompatibility of industry and love. Associated with the Christian notion of charity is an assumption of *spiritual* equality among men which the colliers "literalize" to demand *material* equality, a sort of equality impossible in industry, where authority and hierarchy are operating principles. Indeed, authority and hierarchy are the bases upon which Crich has built his image as "a father of loving kindness and sacrificial benevolence" (258). In Lawrence's handling of the exposition, the ease with which the meaning of *charity* collapses into *equality* and that of *equality* into *desire for chaos* indicates the fragility, indeed the emptiness, of the notion of love upon which the elder Crich builds his career and his self-image.

Like his father, Gerald believes in the reality of certain words and in the reality of the image created through them. One such word is *harmony,* a term that Gerald concludes is "the essential secret of life": "He did not define to himself at all clearly what harmony was. The word pleased him, he felt he had come to his own conclusions. And he proceeded to put his philosophy into practice by forcing order into the established world, translating the mystic word harmony into the practical word organisation" (220). The process by which "harmony" is translated into "organisation" provides an analogue to that by which spiritual equality is converted into material equality by the miners.

By treating "the mystic word harmony" as a synonym for "the practical word organisation," Gerald creates the illusion of spiritual or moral sanction for his industrial activities, for his modernization of the mines. He also shows astonishing disregard for the change in meaning that must accompany the change in context. The narrator's remarks about Gerald's reorganization of his father's business stress the disastrous consequences of this disregard for context: "It was the first step in the undoing, the first great phase of chaos, the substitution of the mechanical principle for the organic . . . . It was pure organic disintegration and pure mechanical organisation. This was the first and finest state of chaos" (223–24). The "substitution of the mechanical principle for the organic," the narrator makes clear, necessarily produces what might seem—at least to Gerald—startling reversals in the meanings of terms like *integration* and *disintegration*. The equation established by the narrator—mechanical integration = organic disintegration (chaos)—stands in distinct contrast to Gerald's equation—mechanical integration (organization) = harmony—and makes it plain that Gerald worships chaos under the name of *harmony*.

Love is another "mystic word" for Gerald, a term to which he clings in an attempt to endow his life with value and meaning. In "Gladiatorial," he expounds his belief in love even as he admits that he has never experienced it: "'I always believed in love—true love. But where does one find it nowadays? . . . I've never felt it myself—not what I should call love. I've gone after women—and been keen enough over some of them. But I've never felt *love*. I don't believe I ever felt as much *love* for a woman, as I have for you—not *love*'" (267–68). Gerald's almost incantatory repetition confirms the hollowness of the concept for him, suggesting that he must attempt to give it reality or substance through verbal handling or manipulation.

Because *love* is a "mystic word" for Gerald, Gudrun is able, at the end of the novel, to enact a kind of annihilation of him through destroying the word *love*. Her verbal perversity at the beginning of "Snowed Up" unmasks her "love," disclosing her need to dominate. After insisting that she never loved Gerald and forcing him to state that he never loved her, she turns and attempts to wheedle and coax him into saying that he does love her: "'Say it, even if it isn't true—say it, Gerald, do'" (434). Gerald complies, "in real agony, forcing the words out": "He stood as if he had been beaten. . . . The darkness seemed to be swaying in waves across his mind. . . . It seemed to him he was degraded at the very quick, made of no account" (434). The parallel between the degradation of the word *love* in this scene and Gerald's own sense of degradation exposes the degree to which Gerald identifies his being with certain sacrosanct words.

Thus Gerald's fate exposes the fallacy of belief in the substantial reality of the word. The repetitions of the word *love* throughout the text underscore the point in a kind of differential dance that also illustrates an important way in which the novel delineates character: through the characters' differing relations to the same word. In pleading with Gerald to lie about his love for her, for example, Gudrun aligns herself with him as one of those characters who places her faith in the reality of the word and the created image. She uses words not only to dominate others, but also to shield herself from her painful, essential awareness that "Everything was intrinsically a piece of irony..." (409). The effort to shield herself is plain, for example, in a scene in "Continental" where she exclaims, quite seriously, to Ursula: "'You above everybody can't get away from the fact that love, for instance, is the supreme thing...'" (429). The hollowness of Gudrun's words is insinuated subtly through her exclamation's echoing of her earlier remark that one gets "the greatest joy of all" (428) out of lovely stockings!

But she clings to the notion of love almost as tenaciously as Gerald. Despite the pleasures offered by her relationship with Loerke—"the highest satisfaction in the nerves, from the queer interchange of half-suggested ideas, looks, expressions and gestures" (439)—she is "rather offended" ("Did he not think her good-looking then?" [450]) by his debunking of love: "'L'amour, l'amore, die Liebe—I detest it in every language. Women and love there is no greater tedium.... I would give everything, everything, all your love for a little companionship in intelligence'" (450). Loerke exercises over Gudrun the same sort of power that she exercises over Gerald in forcing him to lie about his love. "'It *does not matter,* it does not matter... this love, this amour, this *baiser,*'" Loerke asserts; and Gudrun, "gone pale," agrees in "a rather high, vehement voice" (451) that reveals her rising panic.

These scenes generate their meaning partly in their relation to—and their difference from—earlier scenes involving Birkin and Ursula. Gudrun, in wondering, "Did he not think her good-looking, then?" mentally echoes Ursula's response to Birkin's dissociation from her in "Mino": "'But don't you think me good-looking?' [Ursula persists] in a mocking voice" (138). Gudrun's self-mockery in "Snowed Up" underscores the fundamental cynicism of her relation with Loerke while Ursula's mockery of Birkin constitutes an authentic effort to test and qualify his notions. In the same scene, Ursula's pleading with Birkin to say that he loves her provides another parallel with a difference that enables us to make the same distinction.

Then there is the difference between Birkin's surrender to Ursula's pleading and Gerald's surrender to Gudrun's. Perhaps the reader need not contrast the scene in "Snowed Up" with that in "Mino" to understand that Birkin and Ursula use language to communicate while Gerald and Gudrun use it to manipulate; that story is told over and again in the novel. But by reinforcing the point through such analogous scenes, the text stresses the importance of context and of minute differences in reading human character as well as in reading verbal texts.

Another such parallel, the one between Birkin's state of "abstract earnestness" in "Mino" and Gerald's "strange, scarcely conscious" state at the end of "Continental" draws our attention to a shared tendency in Gerald and Birkin, the tendency to use—or rather abuse—the mind to avoid self-knowledge. In the early scene, Birkin lectures Ursula on the "strange conjunction" (139) that he wants with her. "[M]oved outside of himself" when she enters the room, "agitated and shaken, a frail, unsubstantial body" (136), he lectures her "in a voice of pure abstraction" and hangs "suspended finely and perfectly in this extremity" (137); he scarcely heeds what Ursula says for he is "talking to himself" (139). At the end of "Continental," Gerald and Birkin speak for the last time. Gerald looks "into the distance, with the small-pupilled, abstract eyes of a hawk," "his eyes fixed, looking like a mask used in ghastly religions of the barbarians," "speaking as if in a trance, verbal and blank," "blank before his own words," "hardly responsible for what he said" (430–31).

The two scenes parody the notion of spontaneous, creative utterance, but do so to different ends. Birkin's behavior in "Mino" presents us with a parody of that condition for which he yearns—the condition of being "beyond love, [in] a naked kind of isolation" (137). It appears that he must verbally empty himself of abstractions about human connectedness before he can emotionally or physically "connect" with Ursula, and thus his speechifying becomes a kind of unclogging of the channels of self-awareness and communication. The scene in "Continental" presents us with a travesty of the path of creative utterance as Lawrence conceives it: while Gerald's words about Gudrun in this scene seem to emanate directly from his unconscious, their import never seems to touch him. The shift in the level of his discourse from the ordinary "level of trivial occurrence" (28) to that "of rhapsody" and "trance" (431) would seem to signify a plunge into deeper awareness. But when he returns to a more ordinary level of discourse he reduces his intense (and accurate) perception of hatred for Gudrun to a mere curiosity: " 'But—how I hate her somewhere! It's curious—' "(431). He is "blank before his own words" in the sense of being disconnected from their meaning (" 'All right and all wrong, don't they become synonymous somewhere?' " [430] he says earlier in the scene) and from the "inner voice" that has uttered the truth—" 'how I hate her.' " Thus Gerald's rhapsody leaves him untouched; in emptying himself of his concrete, sensuous perceptions of Gudrun, he is left with nothing but his "icy skepticism" regarding Birkin's love.

Differential Characterization

One wonders if Gerald's momentary access to his unconscious might signify an emergent capacity for the sort of awareness and openness which has enabled Birkin to create his relation with Ursula. The very parallels that establish the difference between Birkin and Gerald may at the same time provoke bewilderment as to why one character survives and the other does not. The difference between Gerald's inability to surrender himself to Birkin's expression of love ("'I've loved you, as well as Gudrun, don't forget'" [431]) and Birkin's submission to Ursula's tender words of love at the end of "Mino," the difference between Birkin's speaking in "a voice of love and irony, and submission" (146) and Gerald's speaking in "icy skepticism" (431)—these apparently represent all the difference between life and death in Lawrence's novel. But what accounts for *that* difference?

At the same time that *Women in Love* provokes the reader's desire to account for the different fates of Birkin and Gerald, it systematically frustrates any satisfaction of that desire. It does so through what we might call the narrative correlative of *pure difference,* the testing against each other, through Birkin and Gerald, of two different conceptions of character and fate. F. H. Langman has written that "Birkin is active and free, Gerald is passive and bound. The effect is of a narrative written from different points of view. Gerald is looked at as fixed and finite, the doomed figure of classical tragedy, Birkin is fluent and immeasurable, the existential hero of the modern novel" (199). The novel seems to place highest value upon the open, exploratory attitude toward life embodied in Ursula and Birkin and in their creative direction of energy toward the achievement of their relationship, but to attempt to judge Gerald and Gudrun by this set of values is to confront a serious problem for they are presented as unaware that the choices open to Birkin and Ursula are open to them—or as incapable of redirecting their lives. The novel vigorously insists upon the possibility of choice and change, and equally vigorously insists that no change is possible for Gerald and Gudrun.[5]

The latter insistence emerges not merely through the rhetoric of fatality so noticeable in Lawrence's presentation of the couple, but also through the novel's particularizing Gerald's life in a way that it does not do for any other character. Only Gerald has a specific past with childhood traumas, parental influences, the enthusiasms of youth. We know a little about the Brangwen parents—and are provided with hints of antagonism between the father and the daughters; but even if we admit information from *The Rainbow,* we do not have the kind of case history of Ursula that we have of Gerald. And as the novel begins, Birkin has a job, four hundred a year, some connections in London, and a dying relationship with Hermione—but otherwise no past.

If, as Langman argues, the closed story—Gerald's story—defines its own moral within the context of a "larger complexity"—the open story of Birkin (184), it is equally true that the specificity of Gerald's history provides a kind of "larger complexity" missing from Birkin's story—the so-called open story. To the extent that Gerald can be seen as a representative man—conditioned by the past, society, and forces over which he has no control—the analogies between him and Birkin stress the difficulty of Birkin's quest. But the double perspective mentioned by Langman prevents us from any final evaluation or placing of Birkin and Gerald because of our awareness of an absence of conditions in each case that obtain in the other. If Birkin's choice to change the direction of his life implies the possibility of change for Gerald also, the complex rendering of powerful unconscious forces at work in Gerald argues against that possibility. Our awareness of the complexity of Gerald's case—and of the lack of corresponding detail in the representation of Birkin and Ursula—may provoke us to question Birkin and Ursula's freedom—or to feel that Lawrence has not sufficiently dramatized their moral achievement.

The difficulty may be stated in other terms. If what Birkin shares with the other characters in the novel constitutes a common ground against which his singularity or individuality may emerge, it also provides a counterthrust to the claims that the novel makes for his singleness. As Leo Bersani has written, "From the point of view of traditional fiction, these transparent analogies subvert a desirable diversity of character and plot.... [They] undermine an explicit credo of singleness" (178). What, indeed, do we find "in" Birkin that we do not find in others in his world? Birkin's "singleness" is a quality he shares with Loerke and Winifred Crich (Bersani 176), and in fact his singularity is called into question in all sorts of ways from the very beginning. His intimacy with Hermione Roddice, which is the first thing we learn of him, is *one* of "various intimacies of mind and soul" (10) that she holds with "various men of capacity." And Birkin himself is *"one* of the school inspectors of the county" (10, emphasis added). He seems to have evolved a unique and clever way of defending his uniqueness:

> His nature was clever and separate, he did not fit at all in the conventional occasion. Yet he subordinated himself to the common idea, travestied himself.
> He affected to be quite ordinary, perfectly and marvellously commonplace. And he did it so well, taking the tone of his surroundings, adjusting himself quickly to his interlocutor and his circumstance, that he achieved a versimilitude of ordinary commonplaceness that usually propitiated his onlookers for the moment, disarmed them from attacking his singleness. (14–15).

Yet such behavior is typical of members of Hermione's circle, where, as Gudrun explains, " 'the really chic thing is to be so absolutely ordinary, so perfectly commonplace and like the person in the street, that you really are a masterpiece of humanity, not the person in the street actually, but the artistic creation of her' " (44).

When Birkin comes down the aisle with Hermione—"expressionless, neutralised, possessed by her as if it were his fate beyond question" (16–17)—he seems nulled while Hermione wears a "rapt, triumphant look" (16). Not only does his possession by Hermione clash with the assertions of his clever, separate nature; the dynamics of their relation, as imaged here, resemble those of Gerald and Gudrun near the end of the novel: "always it was this eternal see-saw, one destroyed that the other might exist, one ratified because the other was nulled" (436). Further undercutting the notion of Birkin's singleness is his affinity with Mrs. Crich in the second chapter, where the two "[confer] together like traitors, like enemies within the camp of other people" (18). When in conversation with Mrs. Crich, Birkin says of people, that they "don't really matter. . . . They jingle and giggle. It would be much better if they were just wiped out. Essentially, they don't exist, they aren't there" (19), his words recall Gudrun's earlier reaction to the giggling, gaping, gossiping inhabitants of Beldover: "She would have liked them all annihilated, cleared away, so that the world was left clear for her" (7).

Such repetitions do, as Bersani has argued in speaking of "frictional characterization" in *Women in Love,* "serve the most finely differentiating activity" (179). Gudrun's desire to see the landscape cleansed of her inferiors arises from too great a degree of self-consciousness while Birkin's remarks arise from a vision of what people might be if they took themselves seriously. His travesty of the "common idea" implies a level of critical awareness absent from the "chic" artistic creation of the "absolutely ordinary." And even if he has not, at the beginning of the novel, eluded the grasp of Hermione, he makes conscious efforts to break free from her while Gerald, even at the very end of the novel, thinks "he would never be gone, since in being near [Gudrun], even, he felt the quickening, the going forth in him, the release" (437). Or take an example not yet mentioned, the numerous conversations on love and marriage in which almost all the characters indulge.[6] This sequence of episodic repetitions reminds us of a ground of common concern against which all the characters act, the concern with sexual relationship as a means of making things "centre" (50) for the individual.[7] At the same time, however, the scenes dramatize the characters' different capacities (or incapacities) for emotional surrender and commitment, for surrender of that "ferocity of . . . idea" that one critic attributes to Lawrence himself (Bayley 27).

Lawrence's own ferocity of idea may seem to govern the episodic repetitions or pairings of analogous scenes in *Women in Love,* so neatly do they counterpoint or seem to comment upon each other in parts of the novel. Such pairings have led one critic to claim that the structure of the novel comes to seem, upon repeated rereadings, "almost too tidy, too symmetrical" (Rudrum 241) and another to compare the novel's form to "an artfully designed and patterned dance" (Ford 208–9). Especially clustering near the center of the novel is a group of chapters in which artfully paired scenes firmly establish the important differences between Ursula and Birkin and Gerald and Gudrun.[8] For example "Mino" and "Water-Party" contain parallel love scenes in which conflict leads to an admission of love. In the former, Ursula challenges Birkin's notions about love; an accession of peace and concord follows their argument. But in the latter, Gudrun wordlessly challenges Gerald by striking him in the face; his admission of love, immediately following her blow, is a tacit commitment to a relationship the essence of which is struggle or opposition.

Scenes in "Rabbit" and "Moony" are similarly paired. Ford has written that

> the generally admired scene in which Gudrun and Gerald subdue a rabbit is especially effective in making us sense the perverse quality of one relationship and in preparing us for the contrasting scene in the chapter succeeding it in which Ursula watches Birkin shattering the moon's image. On both occasions a vigorous conflict in the relationship between a man and a woman is brought before us, but one conflict ends in a friendly pact while the other with a pact Lawrence calls 'a mutual hellish recognition.' (210)

Birkin's decision later in "Moony" to marry Ursula is, furthermore, a repudiation of those "abhorrent mysteries" (234) to which Gerald and Gudrun subconsciously commit themselves in "Rabbit." For Birkin's decision to "make a definite pledge, enter into a definite communion" (247) is, he believes, a way of refusing "the long African process of purely sensual understanding" (246) (associated with Gudrun) and the "mystery of ice-destructive knowledge, snow-abstract annihilation" (246) (associated with Gerald). And, as we have seen, the paired consummations in "Excurse" and "Death and Love" seal the differences between the two couples.

Or seem to. Finally, it is possible to argue, these techniques of differential characterization have the peculiar effect of questioning the very possibility that they assert, the possibility of a "final" or absolute self. If everything we find in Birkin is something that we find in another character and yet somehow different, his individuality then can be said to be constituted only by difference. We may not understand in realistic terms what the difference is, but the text's assertions of difference—or gestures in the direction of such assertion—ultimately constitute a claim for the differential nature of the self. And yet, such is the dialogic[9]—the self-questioning dynamic of the novel— that this assertion calls for a rejoinder that echoes Birkin's final words in the novel: "'I don't believe that.'"

Indeed the novel is permeated with powerful rejoinders to the claims of the differential metaphysic informing *Women in Love*. Not only is there the logocentric impulse represented by literalization, but there are the spectacular symbolic scenes which, as David J. Gordon has written, generate "a symbolic energy far out of proportion to the purpose of furthering the narrative" (*D. H. Lawrence as a Literary Critic* 49).[10] And finally there is the value that the novel assigns to voicing.

Voicing and the Dialogic of *Women in Love*

The very tortuousness and absurdity of some of Birkin's speeches are clues that the verbal process being dramatized may be as important as the content of the speeches. For example, in "Mino," when Birkin offers to Ursula his theory of "star-equilibrium," he expounds the idea for what amounts to eleven pages in the novel and does so using a bewildering array of abstractions like "mystic," "impersonal," "final," "strange," and "conjunction" to mention only a few. His verbosity is dramatic evidence that he is attempting to talk about love without benefit of the language ordinarily used to do so, that he is attempting to work himself out of a conceptual and verbal prison—"a limited, false set of concepts" (34); it is also evidence that utterance is essential to his sense of self.

Conceptually, Birkin succeeds only in creating new prisons for himself when he talks. The reductiveness of his talk and what Ursula calls his "ridiculous, mean effacement into a Salvator Mundi and a Sunday-school teacher, a prig of the stiffest type" (122) become apparent in "Mino" when Mino enters the scene to spring repeatedly upon and cuff a stray female cat lurking in the garden. Birkin concocts an allegory out of this tussle: to Ursula's claim that Mino is a bully, Birkin responds that Mino wants to bring the female "into a pure, stable equilibrium, a transcendent and abiding *rapport* with the single male" (142). The rigidity and indeed the absurdity of this interpretation are made plain through the narration of the episode which shows Mino's dignity and lordliness to be signs of the cat's otherness—its separateness from the human race—not signs, as Birkin would have it, of superiority over the female stray. Thus Birkin has substituted a new set of restrictive concepts for the old, and all of his arguing fails to release him from the prison of conceptual thought. Ursula's perception of his basic self-mistrust finally deflates his overblown verbiage: "'You don't really want this conjunction,'" she says; "'otherwise you wouldn't talk so much about it, you'd get it'" (144).

One might reasonably ask what all the talk accomplishes for Birkin. The rest of the chapter proclaims a victory for Ursula, who still believes in "love." Since Birkin has been "wearied out"—silenced in fact—by his own verbosity, she talks quietly and with feeling about her own experiences. Her direct expression of emotion in this scene seems to modify Birkin's stance with regard to the word *love* so that at the end of the chapter he speaks wistfully and concessively in her language: "'I love you then—I love you'" (146). The intellectual oppositions between Ursula and Birkin remain unresolved in "Mino," and speech seems finally to give way to passion, a pattern that is repeated in "Water-Party." There, after an exhausting process of thinking and speaking, Birkin yields to passion for Ursula, abandoning words with relief and thinking, " 'I was becoming... nothing but a word-bag' " (180).

Thus it seems that if words are incapable of effecting that "strange conjunction" that Birkin wants, still some part of him that relies on words must assert itself before that other part, which is capable of passion, can come into being. In this sense, the thinking, speaking self liberates the passionate self, a pattern most memorably dramatized in "Moony," where the famous scene in which Birkin stones the pond can be taken as an image of Birkin as preacher and of the effect of his verbalizing throughout the book. At the beginning of the chapter, Birkin is "talking disconnectedly to himself" (238) as he wanders in the moonlight by the shore of Willey Pond. He is witnessed by Ursula but unaware of her presence as he speaks:

> "You can't go away," he was saying. "There *is* no away. You only withdraw upon yourself."
> He threw a dead flower-husk on to the water.
> "An antiphony—they lie, and you sing back to them. There wouldn't have to be any truth, if there weren't any lies. Then one needn't assert anything—" (280–81)

Birkin not only talks to himself; he talks about talking—verbal assertion—and his attempt to withdraw from humanity, which uses language falsely and destructively. " 'You sing back to them' " is self-condemnation, a reflection on his own participation in the withering, life-denying mentality of his world.

As his frustration mounts, he begins to cast stones at the reflection of the moon, much as he has all along been throwing out his evolving philosophy to Ursula; and the imagery of this part of the scene recapitulates the dialectic of his relationship with her. The alternations of giving over of self and of hostility and withdrawal are imaged in the reflection of the moon as it explodes, flying asunder, then "draws itself together with strange violent pangs" then "get[s] stronger, reasserting itself" with its "rays . . . hastening in thin lines of light, to return to the strengthened moon" (239). The movements of the reflection of the moon also figure forth the action at the end of the chapter when Ursula, angered by Birkin's "bullying" of her, "recoils" upon herself, becoming "hard and self-completed like a jewel" (298). Despite the onslaughts of Birkin's talk, Ursula remains inviolable as the moon.

The imagery of the pond-stoning scene hints at the impossibility of achieving a union of two people through speech as it is often used in the world of the novel—as an instrument of self-assertion, dominance, and aggression. The only response that Birkin receives to his impassioned harangue of the moon is the "rocking of hollow noise" (240) created by the stones he casts into the water. His verbal and physical violence seem, in fact, to be a working out of all the destructive tendencies that propel his speech up to this point, so his final satisfaction with the inarticulate response of "sharp, regular flashes of sound" (240) anticipates his recognition later in the chapter that Ursula's acceptance of him "must happen beyond the sound of words. It was merely ruinous to try to work her by conviction" (242).

Ursula's anger at Birkin in the early part of "Excurse" is the counterpart of his display of feeling in "Moony." Just as he hurled curses at the moon and flung stones across the surface of the pond, she hurls curses at him and flings in the mud the rings that he has given to her. When finally after her anger dissipates she presents him with a flower, it is her version of the proposal that Birkin offered her at the end of "Moony." The language of rebirth pervading the rest of the chapter suggests that these scenes of verbal violence dramatize a kind of "breaking a way through" an old self for each of the characters: Birkin's body is "awake with a simple, glimmering awareness . . . like a thing that is born . . . into a new universe" (304) and Ursula's face is "like a flower, a fresh, luminous flower, glinting faintly with the dew of the first light" (305). But if impassioned speech has allowed these characters to slough off old selves—the overzealous preacher in Birkin and the believer in old-fashioned romantic love in Ursula—their intercourse, in their newness, occurs "as if there were no speech in the world" (305).

In "Excurse," silence becomes the ground of communication between the two, and after that chapter Birkin does not appear again to any appreciable extent in his role as preacher or "word-bag," nor do he and Ursula engage in any more talk of love until the final pages of the novel where Birkin grieves over the love he never had from his friend, Gerald. Thus we are finally forced to ask if the pattern of debate between Birkin and Ursula constitutes a restoration of speech to a healthy place in human relationships or a repudiation of speech. While the dialectic of their courtship implicitly argues that there is a creative relation between speech and feeling and speech and self-realization, Lawrence seems to find it increasingly difficult in *Women in Love* (and in the novels that come afterwards) to dramatize those creative relationships: not only do Birkin and Ursula get tired of talking; they attempt to break with their entire known world, rejecting membership in any community and thus abandoning many forms of experience for which speech is necessary.

Birkin's problematic relation to words may be read as an implicit commentary on Lawrence's struggle with language as he attempts to communicate "new" forms of experience that have "no social objectification,"[11] but we must remember that novels are not spoken but written. *Women in Love* dramatizes the limitations of language conceived as speech or voicing, that is, of language conceived as immediately expressive of essence and as the guarantee of self-present meaning. But the novel also explores the creative potential of dialogue. And it is the dialogic of organic and differential metaphysics that generates the textual energy of Lawrence's masterpiece.

Epilogue

I have focused on *Sons and Lovers, The Rainbow,* and *Women in Love* because of all Lawrence's works they have challenged and rewarded me the most. They have done so partly because they embody the tensions that are the subject of this book: because we can witness in them an increasingly powerful "essential criticism" of the organic theory of being that informs them. I have not meant, however, to suggest that the self-questioning energies of Lawrence's language are confined to the works I examine. One might expect to find those dynamics wherever Lawrence writes figuratively—and that, of course, is almost everywhere.

Some recent studies of Lawrence in fact point in the direction of extending my thesis to the works following *Women in Love.* Lydia Blanchard's study of *Lady Chatterley's Lover,* "Lawrence, Foucault, and the Language of Sexuality," directly engages the paradoxical awareness that I find at the heart of Lawrence's writing: an awareness of the way in which language screens us from the reality it discloses. According to Blanchard, Lawrence's last novel embodies a tension "between the need to rescue sexuality from secrecy, to bring it into discourse, and the simultaneous recognition that the re-creation of sexuality in language must always, at the same time, resist language" (33).

In looking at the way in which Lawrence both creates "a language of the feelings" and "call[s] into question the adequacy of that language" (31), Blanchard employs an approach that is closer to the kind of reading I have done than the approaches of Daniel Albright and Avrom Fleishman, whose readings tend to adhere to the organicist and "formalist norm of commensurability of form and content" (Fleishman 171). Both of these critics have nonetheless produced readings that draw our attention to the differential play of language in the later novels. Fleishman closely examines the narrative styles of *St. Mawr* in order to argue that Lawrence's late works are written "in a complex and commanding style" (176) that puts into play "all [the] double-voiced, dialogical situations" (169) outlined by Mikhail Bakhtin's famous

"Discourse Typology in Prose." Albright points us to "a device which never appears in the novels published before 1920: Lawrence will take a word or a metaphor and play with it for a paragraph or even longer, twist it, overliteralize it, make a succession of puns, rhymes, jokes" (51); in so doing, Albright claims, Lawrence is "surrendering to the devil"; "by manipulating corrupt speech, by making it feel even queasier than it usually does, he is trying to provide a verbal image of a corrupt subject" (51).

No doubt, as Albright and Fleishman claim, Lawrence yearns for a "real" or "unfallen" or "uncorrupt" language—a language commensurate with the reality it expresses; but he never finds it, and I wish to suggest that the late works, like the works I have examined, also question the very possibility of such a language. That questioning is likely represented by verbal devices of the sort that Albright cites. The most notorious example of that device is a chapter in *Kangaroo,* "Harriet and Lovat at Sea in Marriage," in which "a single figure of speech . . . is toyed with, pawed, cuffed, squeezed like an accordion" (Albright 51). The chapter preceding this juxtaposes to Lawrence's "queasy" manipulations of the single cliché, "at sea," an expressive lyric description of the sea that focuses on its "disintegrative, elemental language" (K 154). The novel is, among other things, a tissue of references to the sea. What would close examination of the various references *and their relation to each other* reveal? What patterning of literal and metaphoric uses might one find? A kind of dialogue of corrupt and redeemed uses? A literalizing movement? Or another pattern reversing the substantialist movement of literalization that we found in *Women in Love* and *The Rainbow*? And what would the pattern or patterns discovered mean?

Addressing such questions might complement and supplement efforts like those of Judith Ruderman and Cornelia Nixon to understand the nature and sources of Lawrence's disturbing vision in the later works. Ruderman suggests that "the violence" of the so-called authority novels represents an effort to combat "the devouring mother" and "reveals a modern-day Orestes committing what he thinks is justifiable homocide in an effort to return the patriarch to his rightful throne" (21). Nixon links Lawrence's authoritarian thought to a more general antifeminist reaction, suggesting that the antifeminism arises from the threat represented not only by the success of the feminist movement but by Frieda Lawrence's sexual independence (233–34). She writes: "The works written in Lawrence's traditionally recognized leadership period . . . seem to represent in some ways a political sublimation of [homoerotic] ideas he expressed more openly during the war years" (191). Looking at the so-called authority novels from the sort of perspective my study offers enables us to see them also as sublimations of the longing to restore an Absolute—some transcendental signified—the very idea of which has largely been discredited by Lawrence's earlier writings.

Notes

Prologue

1. Daniel J. Schneider has also used such an attitude as a point of departure for his discussion in *D. H. Lawrence: The Artist as Psychologist* 1–2. Though the book is more concerned with psychological than with linguistic elements of Lawrence's work, Schneider's recent article, "Alternatives to Logocentrism in D. H. Lawrence," suggests the value of looking at Lawrence from a deconstructionist point of view. That essay confirms a number of points made in my first chapter.

2. See my discussion of *Apocalypse* in chapter 1 (14–16). Lawrence's echoing of Freud anticipates de Man's remarks about "blotting out the disturbing parts of the work."

3. Robert Kiely, who numbers himself among those who question the opposition, provides a useful survey of critics embracing the dichotomy and critics dissenting from it (237).

Chapter 1

1. Gerald L. Bruns's second chapter, "Energeia: The Development of the Romantic Idea of Language," provides an excellent historical context for this aspect of Lawrence's thought. Two more recent works on romantic discourse expand that context in ways that are illuminating for the study of Lawrence's thought about language: Tilottama Rajan's *Dark Interpreter: The Discourse of Romanticism* and Anne K. Mellor's *English Romantic Irony*.

2. This early version of "The Spirit of Place" originally appeared in *English Review*, November 1918.

3. The paradox here is neatly summarized by Kenneth Burke: "In being a link between us and the nonverbal, words are by the same token a screen separating us from the nonverbal . . ." (5).

4. The context and implications of Saussure's statement are usefully elaborated by Jameson 11–22.

5. My description of the organic self draws upon Walter Benn Michaels's description of the Cartesian subject (394–95). The two models of the self that I present of course participate in the philosophical debate between nominalism and realism.

6. See, for example, Moynahan 41–42.

7. See Sagar, *D. H. Lawrence: A Calendar of His Works* 54–56, 58, 60–66, for details concerning the chronology of the Hardy study, *The Rainbow*, and "The Crown," which follows the novel and which I discuss later in this chapter.

8. One critic who recognizes this tendency is Colin Clarke, who discusses "the tendency of images of dissolution to polarise, pointing to the possibilities of both disembodiment and decay" (32) and thus breaking down certain oppositions like the heavenly and the demonic. Also see Gamini Salgado on the language of *Women in Love*: "it is not long before what look like oppositions turn out to be variations" (99). A more orthodox view of Lawrentian dualism is presented by H. M. Daleski 18–41.

Chapter 2

1. In writing of "the glow of something wonderful and lost, remembered vividly" (382), John A. Taylor singles out this feature of the novel as a source of the book's power over readers.

2. Daniel A. Weiss's psychoanalytic discussion of "Miriam's contribution to the composite mother image" (48-49) leads to this conclusion as does Shirley Panken's discussion of Paul's "fear of separation from and loss of love of his mother" (580).

3. See Martz 353. Also Weiss argues that in such passages Paul attributes to Miriam "his [own] infantile need for love" (52).

4. Martz's essay presents that counterinterpretation at length (343-64). Though Gavriel Ben-Ephraim does not cite Martz, his reading overlaps with Martz's—and mine—in a number of details.

5. Cf. Gavriel Ben-Ephraim: "The careful examination of narrative dichotomy in Lawrence reveals that the function of the teller is to subvert the integrated identity of woman and evade the failed autonomy of man" (23).

6. *Hudson Review* 1: 77; rpt. in O'Connor 19. Less harsh in his judgment of Lawrence is Emile Delavenay, whose criticisms of *Sons and Lovers* and whose defenses of Jessie Chambers place him in the same camp as Schorer. See *D. H. Lawrence* 119–21 and "D. H. Lawrence and Jessie Chambers: The Traumatic Experiment."

7. See, for example, Dorothy Van Ghent 298, 309–310; Mark Spilka 45, 51, 56, 66; Keith Sagar, *The Art of D. H. Lawrence*, 25–32; and Kate Millett 251–54.

8. The "metaphysics" Bedient has in mind, however, centers on an ideal of "mystic self-dispersal" in "a universe of apotheosized feeling" (118) which enters Lawrence's writing with this novel.

Chapter 3

1. The novel's double perspective on the characters has been the subject of critical commentary by Eugene Goodheart 120, David Cavitch 53, S. L. Goldberg 424, and Edward Engelberg 107. Eliseo Vivas's criticism that Lawrence "fails to integrate the experience of his characters with their external world" (217) is directed precisely at the split or doubleness that so many readers find in the characterization in the novel; and the doubleness is, one might argue, a product of what Mark Spilka has called a "strange double criticism . . . of the flesh as well as the spirit" (94) in *The Rainbow*.

2. Lawrence's "Study of Thomas Hardy" can in fact cast a good deal of indirect illumination on the issues that concern us in *The Rainbow*. In straining "to see what man had done in fighting outwards toward knowledge . . . to hear how he uttered himself in his conquest, [their] deepest desire [hanging] on the battle that [they] heard, far off, being waged on the edge of the unknown" (3), the Brangwen women embody impulses identified in the Hardy study as "male," impulses Lawrence designates as the Will-to-Motion and which he

associates with Knowing. Conversely, the ancestral Brangwen men embody "female" impulses; *The Rainbow* gives us a vivid picture of what Lawrence's "pollyanalytic" calls the Will-to-Inertia (associated with Being as opposed to Knowing) by offering the following description of the Brangwen men at home: "the men sat by the fire in the house where the women moved about with surety, and the limbs and the body of the men were impregnated with the day, cattle and earth and vegetation and the sky, the men sat by the fire and their brains were inert, as their blood flowed heavy with the accumulation from the living day" (3).

In the "Study of Thomas Hardy," Lawrence writes "that the division between male and female is arbitrary, for the purpose of thought" (P 448). By reversing the poles of the opposition in the opening pages of *The Rainbow* he thus stresses that "male" and "female" are not gender designations in his writing so much as they are a way of indicating opposing forces within the individual. An *ideal* presented in the Hardy study is a balance of these impulses, but Lawrence's description there of actual balance is one of almost bovine contentment, one where the value of balance seems equivocal: "A man who is well balanced between male and female, in his own nature, is, as a rule, happy, easy to mate, easy to satisfy, and content to exist. It is only a disproportion or a dissatisfaction, which makes the man struggle into articulation" (P 460).

Our sense that disproportion may be more desirable than balance is strengthened when we realize that such a man is a rarity and his innate balance is not the unattainable ideal balance that Lawrence sees, in the Hardy study, as the goal of all creative human interaction: "Since there is never to be found a perfect balance or accord of the two Wills, but always one triumphs over the other, in life, according to our knowledge, so must the human effort be to recover the balance, to symbolize and so to possess that which is missing" (P 447). The "struggle into articulation," "the human effort . . . to symbolize and so to possess that which is missing"—these are what we know in life and what Lawrence most centrally concerns himself with in *The Rainbow*; these efforts in fact constitute "the religious effort of man" (P 447). That "there is never to be found a perfect balance or accord of the two Wills" may account for the oscillation of values not only in the beginning of the novel but throughout it, a prime example of which is the pervasive ambivalence toward language and culture.

3. As we might expect, the ambivalence makes its way into the criticism. We find F. R. Leavis, on the one hand, writing that the theme of the novel is "the urgency, and the difficult struggle, of the higher human possibilities to realize themselves" (113) and Marguerite Beede Howe, on the other hand, writing that "Succeeding generations descend from a higher, happier, integrated state to a condition of increasing disharmony and disorder, albeit of higher consciousness also" (35). Aidan Burns briefly discusses the ambivalent place that language holds in the development of the self in *The Rainbow* (52).

4. Another interesting "division" has been noted by Daniel Mark Fogel, one between the third and fourth sentences of the novel: "We note a grammatical oddity, the period between the words *sky* and *So that* falling where conventional practice would call for a comma or a semicolon" (48).

5. The quotation is from Barbara Johnson's translator's introduction to *Disseminations* (ix). Derrida's essay, "Différance," provides a complex, implicative definition of the concept.

6. Two critics who do not underestimate the significance of punning in Lawrence are Garrett Stewart, "Lawrence, 'Being' and the Allotropic Style," and Michael Ragussis in his chapters on *Women in Love*.

7. Cf. Shoshana Felman on Balzac's "Girl with the Golden Eyes": "femininity as real otherness, in Balzac's text, is uncanny in that it is not the opposite of masculinity, but *that which subverts the very opposition of masculinity and femininity*" (42). Felman's entire essay has

much to teach readers of *The Rainbow* concerning the metalinguistic dimension of the sexual relations Lawrence portrays. Another work directing our attention to this dimension of Lawrence is Catherine Stearns's "Gender, Voice, and Myth: The Relation of Language to the Female in D. H. Lawrence's Poetry."

8. An analogous collapsing of an opposition occurs in the "Study of Thomas Hardy" when, after establishing the dichotomy of motion and inertia, Lawrence writes, "there is no such thing as rest. There is only infinite motion..." (P 448).

9. To look at Ursula's encounters with Skrebensky in this way is to confirm Stephen J. Miko's remark that "it seems that Lawrence is experimenting with his ontology through these scenes" (173).

10. Robert Langbaum is typical of commentators writing about the concept of the self in *The Rainbow*. He writes that Lawrence "reconstitutes the romantic assertion that the self remains continuous in all its phases" (316). I argue that such a view represents only part of the story.

11. For a detailed description of the composition process, see Mark Kinkead-Weekes, "The Marble and the Statue." He writes: "*The Rainbow* was almost certainly written backwards; the story of Tom and Lydia being the last to take shape, with the others being filled out thematically against its perspective" (384). The point is confirmed by Charles L. Ross's discussion of the earliest surviving fragment of *Sisters* (15–19).

12. Michael Squires discusses the use of rhetorical signals that create some of the effects I examine here (137-40).

13. For other treatments of the stylistic issues raised by this passage see Frank Glover Smith 26–27 and Daleski 78.

14. Engelberg writes of Anna's "multiplication" of herself through child-bearing (108).

Chapter 4

1. Sybil Jacobson includes this metaphor in her discussion of the paradoxical nature of border imagery in *Women in Love* (60–63).

2. Ragussis asks a similar question to make the same point (178–79). He also presents an interesting discussion of the range of meanings that the text establishes for the term "inhuman" (179).

3. Ragussis examines the way in which the novel dramatizes this assumption (193–97).

4. Critics who have commented on this quality of *Women in Love* include Salgado 97 and David J. Gordon, *"Women in Love* and the Lawrentian Aesthetic" 51.

Chapter 5

1. For another treatment of the novel's concern with contextuality see Ragussis 186 et passim.

2. To say this is to differ with T. H. Adamowski, whose discussion of *Women in Love* and Sartre's *Being and Nothingness* argues that Lawrence sees a self that may know "completion" (349). Again we have an example of the critical habit of granting one theory of being in Lawrence's prose absolute sway.

3. An interesting extension of the differential method of reading required by the novel is offered by Michael L. Ross, who looks at correspondences between *Women in Love* and

The Rainbow, arguing that the two works "reveal their full depth and complexity only when read in conjunction with one another" (285). A similar assumption informs Janice Hubbard Harris's *The Short Fiction of D. H. Lawrence.*

4. They strike Derek Bickerton in this way. See his attack upon the style of *Women in Love* (61).

5. Alan Rudrum presents a related paradox in remarking that while the inevitability of Gerald's death is essential to Lawrence's conception, so is the idea that this inevitability itself is not inevitable (250).

6. See, for examples, such conversations occurring in "Sisters," "In the Train," "Man to Man," "Gladiatorial," "Threshold," "Woman to Woman," and "Marriage or Not."

7. Cf. Richard Drain: "we might consider the degree to which the characters are involved in a common situation and a common plight" (71).

8. See C. Pirinet, who has called chapters 14 through 20 "une sorte de noyau structural du livre" (143).

9. By using this term I do not mean to draw into this discussion all of the technical distinctions made by Mikhail Bakhtin in his discourse typology, but merely to suggest that the opposition of two theories of being in Lawrence can be viewed as a kind of dialogue.

10. Also see Peter K. Garrett 213 and Eliseo Vivas 281–82 on the force exerted by such symbols.

11. Mark Schorer, *"Women in Love* and Death," *Hudson Review* 6: 39; rpt. in Spilka, *D.H. Lawrence* 54.

Works Cited

Adamowski, T. H. "Being Perfect: Lawrence, Sartre, and Women in Love." *Critical Inquiry* 2 (1975): 345–68.

Albright, Daniel. *Personality and Impersonality: Lawrence, Woolf, and Mann.* Chicago: U of Chicago P, 1978.

Alldritt, Keith. *The Visual Imagination of D. H. Lawrence.* Evanston: Northwestern UP, 1971.

Armin, Arnold. *D. H. Lawrence and America.* London: Linden, 1958.

Bakhtin, Mikhail. "Discourse Typology in Prose." *Readings in Russian Poetics,* trans. L. Metejka and K. Pomorska, pp. 176–96. Cambridge: MIT Press, 1971.

Bayley, John. *The Characters of Love. A Study of the Literature of Personality.* New York: Basic, 1960.

Bedient, Calvin. *Architects of the Self: George Eliot, D. H. Lawrence, and E. M. Forster.* Berkeley: U of California P, 1972.

Ben-Ephraim, Gavriel. *The Moon's Dominion: Narrative Dichotomy and Female Dominance in Lawrence's Earlier Novels.* Rutherford, N.J.: Fairleigh Dickinson UP; London: Associated U Presses, 1981.

Bersani, Leo. *A Future for Astyanax: Character and Desire in the Novel.* Boston: Little, Brown, 1976.

Berthoud, Jacques. *"The Rainbow* as Experimental Novel." *D. H. Lawrence: A Critical Study of the Major Novels and Other Writings,* ed. A. H. Gomme, pp. 53–69. Hassocks, Sussex: Harvester; New York: Barnes, 1978.

Bickerton, Derek. "The Language of *Women in Love." A Review of English Literature* 8 (1967): 56–67.

Blanchard, Lydia. "Lawrence, Foucault, and the Language of Sexuality." *D. H. Lawrence's 'Lady': A New Look at* Lady Chatterley's Lover, ed. Michael Squires and Dennis Jackson, pp. 17–35. Athens: U of Georgia P, 1985.

Bruns, Gerald L. *Modern Poetry and the Idea of Language: A Critical and Historical Study.* New Haven: Yale UP, 1974.

Burke, Kenneth. *Language as Symbolic Action: Essays on Life, Literature and Method.* Berkeley: U of California P, 1966.

Burns, Aidan. *Nature and Culture in D. H. Lawrence.* London: Macmillan, 1980.

Cavitch, David. *D. H. Lawrence and the New World.* New York: Oxford UP, 1969.

Chambers, Jessie. *D. H. Lawrence: A Personal Record by "E. T."* 2nd ed. Ed. J. D. Chambers. New York: Barnes, 1965.

Clarke, Colin. *River of Dissolution: D. H. Lawrence and English Romanticism.* New York: Barnes, 1969.

Culler, Jonathan. *On Deconstruction: Theory and Criticism after Structuralism.* Ithaca: Cornell UP, 1982.

Cushman, Keith. *D. H. Lawrence: The Emergence of the* Prussian Officer *Stories.* Charlottesville: UP of Virginia, 1978.

Daleski, H. M. *The Forked Flame: A Study of D. H. Lawrence.* London: Faber; Evanston: Northwestern UP, 1965.

Delavenay, Emile. "D. H. Lawrence and Jessie Chambers: The Traumatic Experiment." *The D. H. Lawrence Review* 12 (1979): 305-25.

――――. *D. H. Lawrence: The Man and His Work: The Formative Years: 1885-1919.* Trans. Katharine M. Delavenay. Carbondale: Southern Illinois UP, 1972.

de Man, Paul. *Blindness and Insight: Essays in the Rhetoric of Contemporary Criticism.* N. Y.: Oxford UP, 1971.

Derrida, Jacques. "Différance." *Margins of Philosophy,* trans. Alan Bass, pp. 1-27. Chicago: U of Chicago P, 1982.

Drain, Richard. *"Women in Love." D. H. Lawrence: A Critical Study of the Major Novels and Other Writings,* ed. A. H. Gomme, pp. 70-93. Hassocks, Sussex: Harvester; New York: Barnes, 1978.

Engelberg, Edward. "Escape from the Circles of Experience: D. H. Lawrence's *The Rainbow* as Bildungsroman." *PMLA* 78 (1963): 103-13.

Felman, Shoshana. "Rereading Femininity." *Yale French Studies* 62 (1981): 19-44.

Fleishman, Avrom. "He Do the Polis in Different Voices: Lawrence's Later Style." *D. H. Lawrence: A Centenary Consideration,* ed. Peter Balbert and Phillip Marcus, pp. 162-79. Ithaca: Cornell UP, 1985.

Fogel, Daniel Mark. "The Sacred Poem of the Unknown in the Fiction of D. H. Lawrence." *The D. H. Lawrence Review* 16 (1983): 45-57.

Ford, George H. *Double Measure: A Study of the Novels and Stories of D. H. Lawrence.* 1965. New York: Norton Library, 1969.

Freud, Sigmund. *The Standard Edition of the Complete Psychological Works of Sigmund Freud.* Ed. and trans. James Strachey. 24 vols. London: Hogarth, 1964.

Garrett, Peter K. *Scene and Symbol from George Eliot to James Joyce: Studies in Changing Fictional Mode.* Yale Studies in English, vol. 172. New Haven: Yale UP, 1969.

Goldberg, S. L. *"The Rainbow*: Fiddle-Bow and Sand." *Essays in Criticism* 11 (1961): 418-34.

Goodheart, Eugene. *The Utopian Vision of D. H. Lawrence.* Chicago: U of Chicago P, 1963.

Gordon, David J. *D. H. Lawrence as a Literary Critic.* Yale Studies in English, vol. 161. New Haven: Yale UP, 1966.

――――. *"Women in Love* and the Lawrentian Aesthetic." *Twentieth-Century Interpretations of* Women in Love, ed. Stephen J. Miko, pp. 50-60. Englewood Cliffs, N.J.: Prentice, 1969.

Harris, Janice Hubbard. *The Short Fiction of D. H. Lawrence.* New Brunswick: Rutgers UP, 1984.

Hochman, Baruch. *Another Ego: The Changing View of Self and Society in the Works of D. H. Lawrence.* Columbia, S.C.: U of South Carolina P, 1970.

Hough, Graham. *The Dark Sun: A Study of D. H. Lawrence.* London: Duckworth, 1956.

Howe, Marguerite Beede. *The Art of the Self in D. H. Lawrence.* Athens, Ohio: Ohio UP, 1977.

Jacobson, Sybil. "The Paradox of Fulfillment: A Discussion of *Women in Love." The Journal of Narrative Technique* 3 (1973): 53-65.

Jameson, Fredric. *The Prisonhouse of Language: A Critical Account of Structuralism and Russian Formalism.* 1972. Princeton: Princeton UP, 1974.

Johnson, Barbara. *The Critical Difference: Essays in the Contemporary Rhetoric of Reading.* Baltimore: Johns Hopkins UP, 1980.

――――. Translator's Introduction. *Dissemination.* By Jacques Derrida. Chicago: U of Chicago P, 1981.

Kalnins, Mara, ed. *Apocalypse and the Other Writings on Revelation.* By D. H. Lawrence. New York: Cambridge UP, 1980.

Kermode, Frank. *D. H. Lawrence.* Modern Masters Series. N.Y.: Viking, 1973.

Kiely, Robert. *Beyond Egotism: The Fiction of James Joyce, Virginia Woolf, and D. H. Lawrence.* Cambridge, Mass.: Harvard UP, 1980.

Kinkead-Weekes, Mark. "The Marble and the Statue: The Exploratory Imagination of D. H. Lawrence." *Imagined Worlds: Essays on Some English Novels and Novelists in Honour of John Butt,* ed. Maynard Mack and Ian Gregor, pp. 371–418. London: Methuen, 1968.

Langbaum, Robert. *The Mysteries of Identity: A Theme in Modern Literature.* 1977. Chicago: U of Chicago P, 1982.

Langman, F. H. *"Women in Love."* *Essays in Criticism* 17 (1967): 183–206.

Lawrence, D. H. *Apocalypse and the Writings on Revelation.* Ed. Mara Kalnins. The Cambridge Edition of the Works of D. H. Lawrence. New York: Cambridge UP, 1980.

⸻. *Kangaroo.* 1920. New York: Viking, 1960.

⸻. *The Letters of D. H. Lawrence.* Vol. 1: 1901–1913. Ed. James T. Boulton. Vol. 2: 1913–1916. Ed. George J. Zytaruk and James T. Boulton. The Cambridge Edition of the Letters and Works of D. H. Lawrence. New York: Cambridge UP, 1979–1981.

⸻. *Phoenix: The Posthumous Papers of D. H. Lawrence.* Ed. Edward D. McDonald. 1936. New York: Viking, 1968.

⸻. *Phoenix II: Uncollected, Unpublished and Other Prose Works by D. H. Lawrence.* Ed. Warren Roberts and Harry T. Moore. New York: Viking, 1968.

⸻. *Psychoanalysis and the Unconscious and Fantasia of the Unconscious.* 1921, 1922. New York: Viking, 1960.

⸻. *The Rainbow.* 1915. New York: Penguin, 1976.

⸻. *Sons and Lovers.* 1913. New York: Penguin, 1976.

⸻. *Studies in Classic American Literature.* 1923. New York: Viking, 1964.

⸻. *Women in Love.* 1920. New York: Penguin, 1976.

Leavis, F. R. *D. H. Lawrence: Novelist.* 1955. Chicago: U of Chicago P, 1979.

Martz, Louis L. "Portrait of Miriam: A Study in the Design of *Sons and Lovers.*" *Imagined Worlds: Essays on Some English Novels and Novelists in Honour of John Butt,* ed. Maynard Mack and Ian Gregor, pp. 343–69. London: Methuen, 1968.

Mellor, Anne K. *English Romantic Irony.* Cambridge, Mass.: Harvard UP, 1980.

Michaels, Walter Benn. "The Interpreter's Self: Peirce on the Cartesian Subject." *The Georgia Review* 31 (1977): 381–402.

Miko, Stephen J. *Toward Women in Love: The Emergence of a Lawrentian Aesthetic.* Yale Studies in English, vol. 177. New Haven: Yale UP, 1971.

Miller, J. Hillis. "The Critic as Host." *Deconstruction and Criticism.* Ed. Harold Bloom et al. New York: Seabury, 1979. 217–53.

⸻. "Deconstructing the Deconstructors." *Diacritics* 5 (Summer 1975): 24–31.

⸻. *Fiction and Repetition.* Cambridge, Mass.: Harvard UP, 1982.

Millett, Kate. *Sexual Politics.* 1969. New York: Equinox Books–Avon, 1971.

Moynahan, Julian. *The Deed of Life: The Novels and Tales of D. H. Lawrence.* Princeton: Princeton UP, 1963.

Nixon, Cornelia. *Lawrence's Leadership Politics and the Turn Against Women.* Berkeley: U of California P, 1986.

Panken, Shirley. "Some Psychodynamics in *Sons and Lovers*: A New Look at the Oedipal Theme." *Psychoanalytic Review* 61 (1974–75): 571–89.

Pirinet, C. "La Structure symbolique de *Women in Love.*" *Etudes Anglaises* 22 (1969): 138–51.

Potter, Stephen. *D. H. Lawrence: A First Study.* London: Jonathan Cape, 1930.

Ragussis, Michael. *The Subterfuge of Art: Language and the Romantic Tradition.* Baltimore: Johns Hopkins UP, 1978.

Rajan, Tilottama. *Dark Interpreter: The Discourse of Romanticism.* Ithaca: Cornell UP, 1980.

Ross, Charles L. *The Composition of* The Rainbow *and* Women in Love. Charlottesville: U P of Virginia for the Bibliographical Society of the U of Virginia, 1979.

Ross, Michael L. "'More or Less a Sequel'": Continuity and Discontinuity in Lawrence's Brangwensaga." *The D. H. Lawrence Review* 14 (1981): 263-88.

Ruderman, Judith. *D. H. Lawrence and the Devouring Mother: The Search for a Patriarchal Ideal of Leadership.* Durham, N.C.: Duke UP, 1984.

Rudrum, Alan. "Philosophical Implication in *Women in Love.*" *The Dalhousie Review* 51 (1971): 240-50.

Sagar, Keith. *The Art of D. H. Lawrence.* Cambridge: Cambridge UP, 1966.

_____. *D. H. Lawrence: A Calendar of His Works.* Austin: U of Texas P, 1979.

Said, Edward. *Beginnings: Intention and Method.* Baltimore: Johns Hopkins UP, 1975.

Salgado, Gamini. "Taking a Nail for a Walk: On Reading *Women in Love.*" *The Modern English Novel: The Reader, the Writer, and the Work.* Ed. Gabriel Jospovici. New York: Barnes and Noble, 1976.

Saussure, Ferdinand de. *Course in General Linguistics.* Ed. Charles Bally and Albert Sechehaye with Albert Riedlinger. Trans. Wade Baskin. New York: McGraw-Hill, 1966.

Schneider, Daniel J. "Alternatives to Logocentrism in D. H. Lawrence." *The South Atlantic Review* 51. 1 (May 1986): 35-47.

_____. *D. H. Lawrence: The Artist as Psychologist.* Lawrence: UP of Kansas, 1984.

Schorer, Mark. "Technique as Discovery." *Hudson Review* 1 (1948): 67-87. Rpt. in *Forms of Modern Fiction: Essays in Honor of Joseph Warren Beach,* ed. William Van O'Connor, pp. 9-29. 1948; rpt. Bloomington: Midland Books—Indiana UP, 1959. 9-29.

_____. *"Women in Love* and Death." *The Hudson Review* 6 (1953): 34-47. Rpt. in *D. H. Lawrence: A Collection of Critical Essays,* ed. Mark Spilka, pp. 50-60. Twentieth-Century Views. Englewood Cliffs, N.J.: Prentice-Hall, 1963.

Schwarz, Daniel R. "Speaking of Paul Morel: Voice, Unity, and Meaning in *Sons and Lovers.*" *Studies in the Novel* 8 (1976): 255-77.

Smith, Frank Glover. *D. H. Lawrence*: The Rainbow. Studies in English Literature, no. 46. London: Edward Arnold, 1971.

Spilka, Mark. *The Love Ethic of D. H. Lawrence.* Bloomington: Indiana UP, 1955.

Squires, Michael. "Scenic Construction and Rhetorical Signals in Hardy and Lawrence." *The D. H. Lawrence Review* 8 (1975): 125-45.

Stearns, Catherine. "Gender, Voice, and Myth: The Relation of Language to the Female in D. H. Lawrence's Poetry." *The D. H. Lawrence Review* 17 (1984): 233-42.

Steiner, Claude M. *Scripts People Live: Transactional Analysis of Life Scripts.* 1974. New York: Bantam, 1975.

Stewart, Garrett. "Lawrence, 'Being,' and the Allotropic Style." *Towards a Poetics of Fiction: Essays from* Novel: A Forum on Fiction, *1967-76.* Bloomington: Indiana UP, 1977. 331-56.

Taylor, John A. "The Greatness in *Sons and Lovers.*" *Modern Philology* 71 (1974): 380-87.

Tedlock, E. W., Jr. *D. H. Lawrence, Artist and Rebel: A Study of Lawrence's Fiction.* Albuquerque: The U of New Mexico P, 1963.

Tindall, William York. *D. H. Lawrence and Susan His Cow.* New York: Columbia UP, 1939.

Van Ghent, Dorothy. *The English Novel: Form and Function.* 1953. New York: Perennial—Harper, 1967.

Vivas, Eliseo. *D. H. Lawrence: The Failure and Triumph of Art.* 1960. Bloomington: Midland—Indiana UP, 1964.

Weiss, Daniel A. *Oedipus in Nottingham: D. H. Lawrence.* Seattle: U of Washington P, 1962.

Index

"Study of Thomas Hardy," 2, 5, 24–26, 27, 54,
113n7, 114–15n2, 116n8
Style, Lawrence's idiosyncrasies of, 3, 111–12
Symbolic model of language. *See* Language;
and listings under individual novels

Taylor, John A., 114n1
Tindall, William York, 27

Utterance. *See* Language

Van Ghent, Dorothy, 43, 114n7
Vivas, Eliseos, 114n1, 117n10

Weiss, Daniel A., 39, 50, 114n2
Women in Love: the abyss (or void), 75–79,
80, 81, 82, 83, 90, 91; difference, 78,

93–95, 103; differential characterization,
102–6; differential metaphysic, 77, 106,
109; differential model of the self, 93–94,
106; differential nature of language, 93,
94; episodic repetition as differential
dynamic, 93, 106; linguistic differences,
96–98; literalization, 78, 80, 84, 85, 86, 87,
88, 89; multiple meanings, 79, 80–81, 82,
84, 89, 93; organic model of the self (or
"final" self), 94–95, 106, 109; oppositions,
81, 93; repetitions of *go,* 82–88;
repetitions of *love* as differential dynamic,
98–103; self-questioning movement of
language, 79, 81, 89–91; symbolic model
of language, 89; verbal repetition as
differential dynamic, 93, 95, 96–98;
voicing as utterance, 107–9